THE CAPTURE
OF
JACOB (KNEISLE) NICELY
(Revision 2011)

The picture on the front cover is a painting by Andrew Knez Jr. being used with his authorization and permission. The painting is titled "The Abduction of John Tanner". By contacting Mr. Knez at the following address, this painting and many others can be purchased.

Andrew Knez Jr.
(Office and Studio)
P.O. Box 1451
McMurray, PA 15317
(724) 969-3200
Web Site *www.andrewknezjr.com*

I am continuing to expand the information on the (Knusli, Knisely, Knisley) Nicely family tree. If you have a need to reach me (the author) regarding the family tree, my Email address is nicelyguy@msn.com

PENNSYLVANIA

The map of the State of Pennsylvania shows the relative location of the area in which the Nicely Family established their homestead. The map shown below is an exploded view of this area indicating the Four-Mile Run and the capture site in relation to the town of Ligonier, PA.

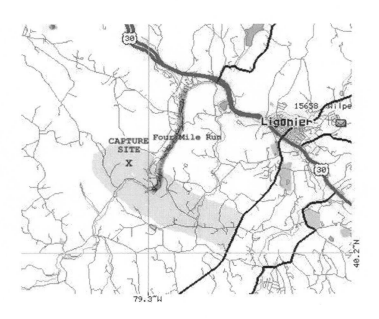

THE INDIAN

CAPTURE

OF

JACOB (KNEISLE) NICELY

Ronald Earl Nicely

For comments, questions, and autographed book purchases
Contact Ronald Earl Nicely directly at
nicelyguy@msn.com

A "Tracing Your Family Roots" video
Featuring the author
about this story can be viewed at
http://www.veoh.com/watch/v20589552BWHDm3y9

This book can also be ordered online at
The Lulu Bookstore at
http://www.lulu.com/shop/shop.ep

or
as an eBook at one of the following
Amazon Kindle
Sony e-Reader
Barnes and Noble Nook
Kobo (Borders) e-Reader
Google eBook site.

Print ISBN: 978-1-6251-7342-3
eBook ISBN: 978-1-6251-7341-6

This book is dedicated to the pioneers of the Nicely family for their efforts to relocate and settle our family in this part of Pennsylvania and to all the researchers who have preceded me in gathering and documenting the Knusli (Kneisle) Nicely Family History.

While the following quotation was about the early English settlers, it applies as well to our Swiss ancestors, who traveled across the great ocean and settled in the wilderness.

May not and ought not the children of these fathers rightly say: "Our fathers were Englishmen which came over this great ocean, and were ready to perish in this wilderness."

William Bradford (1590 - 1657), English-born American religious leader and colonist.

Referring to the Pilgrims, after their arrival at Cape Cod. History of Plymouth Plantation, 1620-1647, 1856.

CONTENTS

PREFACE

The story you are about to read has been told and retold many times over since 1775. It was a story that has been passed down from generation to generation. It will seem more like a legend than a true event, but the story is true, with some corrections to the original recorded history in the Westmoreland County History Books regarding names and dates. Most of the Nicely descendents, who were raised in Ligonier Valley in Pennsylvania, had the story repeated to them many times, by grandparents and parents. Our sense of sadness and the mystery involved in the capture of Jacob left us feeling somewhat incomplete. The family was never sure of what became of Jacob Kneisle and his descendents leaving us with the question of how to begin to find them, since their last or family name was not known. I had been doing research on the family tree for over five years without a clue as to where to look.

On the Whitecrow side of the family, members were told the story of his capture and passed it down through their family historians and knew about Tsu-ka-we's (Jacob's) life and his descendents but had no information on his ancestors or on the location of his birth. Through a very strange set of circumstances, these unknowns were resolved and resulted in a very happy and historic reunion, in 2003, when the descendents of Jacob met with the descendents of his brothers Anthony and Adam Jr. There was surely a force that was guiding this endeavor to help bring our mutual family's quest to a conclusion. God or Ya-Weh led both our families through a series of almost impossible odds to reach each other. It might be compared to the finding of a needle in a haystack.

I will take you through the history of the Mennonite Knusli family as they left Switzerland to journey to Lancaster in America, the area around Ligonier, PA, the history of the Knusli (Kneisle) Nicely family in Ligonier leading up to the capture of Jacob Kneisle. You will learn about Jacob's new name of Tsu-ka-we or Crow living with the Senecas of Sandusky and his descendents, the Whitecrow and Crow families. You will read about the miraculous story that brought the two branches of the family together and the historic meeting that was held in Ligonier Valley in October 2003. I hope you enjoy reading the story as much as I enjoyed putting it together. I doubt that I will ever be able to express the joyful emotions experienced in living through the events that occurred in late August 2003 through to early October of 2003. Suffice to say it was a once in a lifetime memorable experience that left us all feeling extremely satisfied with the conclusion and with what the future still holds for the reunited family members.

I began this research on my family history with only the curiosity of trying to understand where I came from and to develop an understanding of the type of people my ancestors were and their lives. I have learned and experienced so much more than I had ever anticipated. I have developed a great respect for their efforts, which, unknowing to them, gave to all their descendents the opportunity to grow up in a great country, the USA, with freedoms they could only dream of in their lifetime. They were pioneers in every sense of the word risking their lives for a better way of life for themselves and their families. They were not an exceptional family, just one family out of many who took similar risks for their descendents.

There are so many people to thank for their input that I could not possibly mention them all, but there are some that need to be mentioned. My mother, Florence Rose McDowell Nicely, who gathered and documented a lot of the information on the Anthony Nicely branch of the family tree over many years and gave me the basis for the start of my research work. John Robert (Jack) Nicely and Todd Garrett Pelkey, both descendents of Adam Nicely Jr., passed on to me almost all of the history for the Adam Nicely Jr. branch of the tree. On the Whitecrow side of the Kneisle family, Mary Virginia Scritchfield Wood, a descendent of Tsu-ka-we or Crow as Jacob was know by his Indian name, had been searching for her ancestors for around twenty years and had accumulated information on Crow's descendents. Her information was passed on to Leora Lacie Whitecrow, the wife of Sidney Whitecrow, who became involved a few years back and through the use of the Internet and access to the American Indian history files began to expand the knowledge of Jacob's family. A special thanks goes out to Jake Knisely, who was the link in getting our two family branches together again. Without his efforts this story could not have been told. Since this initial contact Jake and the author completed DNA testing and matched and shortly after that we established a paper trail to our common ancestor Antonius Kristopher Knussli. My thanks also goes to my language consultant and proof-reader Phyllis McCracken Humphreys, a second cousin one generation removed on my mother's side of the family, who spent many hours reading and helping me correct the book's language and structure. I would also like to thank my wife Marian (Chris) Plummer Nicely for her patience, as I spent many hours looking for information and for opening our home to those who came to visit and share the family information.

INTRODUCTION

The Revolutionary War took place during the time period of 1775 through 1783. It was during this period of time that all but one of the capture stories that are included in this book took place. The area around the southwestern part of Pennsylvania was a war zone and was under attack from the British, the Renegade whites, and the Indians. Each group had their own reasons for fighting a war with the Colonists in this area. The British were trying to bring the Colonists back into their control and were leading some of these battles and supplying monetary aide, support and incentives to the other two groups during the War. The Renegade whites were outcasts and appeared to enjoy the havoc they were creating plus the monetary gain they could achieve with payments from the British. The Indians were fighting in defense of their land and for the honor of their people. The Indians were being pushed farther west after being forced out of the eastern section of America. Finally, they decided that they had lost enough land and would be pushed no farther. The settlers in southwest Pennsylvania were fighting to maintain property they had farmed and developed, over a ten to fifteen year period of time, prior to the start of the Revolutionary War. It was a difficult time for all parties.

The resentment that developed for each other led to many incidents that left both sides indicating how bloodthirsty the other sides were. It was evident that all sides had some justification for the fighting that took place. As in all periods of war there are many difficult to explain incidents of brutality, but there are quite often unexplained incidents of kindness. The stories reported in this book include incidents of both brutality and kindness. I'm sure both sides celebrated the victories and abhorred the brutality that occurred.

My interest in presenting the factual history of this area during this time period is to show the atmosphere that created the conditions that led to the capture of Jacob Kneisle. The responsibility fell squarely on the shoulders of all participants involved without blame for any one party or the other. The reason that each of the individuals had for his actions are not known. Today one can only guess at what their reasons might have been. The fear created in people during wartime leads them to do things they would not normally do under peaceful situations. We are also aware that there are people of good moral character and people of weak moral character and we should not place blame on the good for the actions of a few.

We are very thankful that Jacob was treated well and developed into a man and fathered a family. We are also grateful for all the generations that had recorded and passed down the history of their family enabling us to get back together to celebrate the meeting of our family branches after such a long period of separation. It is hoped that the future generations of Adam and Elizabeth Eichert Nicely Sr. will understand the difficulties that these early pioneers faced and survived to give them a chance to exist in our world. We also hope that the story of their lives will bolster the confidence of the individuals reading this story and improve their ability to persevere and survive under even the most difficult circumstances.

I sincerely hope that you will find the story of our family not only interesting but also inspiring.

CHAPTER ONE

The Kneisle Family Moves to America

Since the original writing of the book in 2004, I have been able to locate more information on the family's roots. The Nicely family ancestors were originally from Zurich, Switzerland and were Anabaptist Mennonite farmers with our original named ancestor being Hans Knussli (with an umlaut, two dots above the legs of the u), who was born in 1628. The ancestor who moved to America was Antonius Kristopher Knussli, the son of Hans, who came to America in 1717 with his wife Magdalena Hempstead and at least 8 of his 11 children to Magdalena. The other 3 children we do not have definite information on where they lived or died. It is possible they died during the journey by ship to Philadelphia in America. All 11 children were born before the move to America in 1717 and were Magdalena's children to Antonius. However, later in his life in 1730 at the age of 72 he fathered a 12th child to Elizabeth Yeager. That child was Adam Kneisle Sr., who moved to Ligonier in 1761 and was the ancestor of the Nicely family in the Ligonier, PA area. DNA testing of Ronald Nicely, a descendant of Adam Nicely Sr., and Jake Knisely, a descendant of Johannes Hans Kneisley, one of Antonius's sons to Magdalena, proved to be a 100% DNA match with Antonius being the most likely common ancestor. Adam Sr. and Johannes were both sons of Antonius and were half brothers to each other. The Ligonier family story of an Anthony coming to America in 1730 could not be proved by Philadelphia ship records and current information has proved that information to be incorrect..

Over many years the family, as a result of persecution brought on by their belief in adult baptism, moved from

Zurich to Eggiwill in Switzerland and then to the Alsace area on the border of Germany and France. Anabaptist Mennonites held a strong belief in baptism being performed only on those who were old enough to understand and accept joining the church. The Church of Switzerland decided to have all children baptized at an early age and there was to be no exceptions. The Mennonites would not accept this in their religion and they paid a heavy price for their beliefs. This forced them to hide their religious practices and to disobey the rule of the Church of Switzerland.

Even in Alsace they faced persecution forcing a group of nine Mennonite families to leave the area in 1710 and move to America, in the area near Lancaster, PA. In 1717, one of the original 1710 members, Martin Kendig, returned to the Palinate area in Germany and Alsace and recruited other Mennonites to move to America. Our Knussli family accepted this invitation and their journey followed the Rhine River to Rotterdam, in the Netherlands, then by ship to a British port and then by a British ship to America. The travel time by ship from England to America normally took from seven to twelve weeks, sometimes longer. Only British ships were permitted to land legally at American ports, prior to the Revolutionary War. This was the typical route of travel for Swiss and German immigrants to America in that period of time. They and others by the names of Andreas Kauffman who married Elizabeth Knussli and Isaac Kauffman who married Anna Knussli, Michael Miller who married Barbara Knussli, John Witmer, Hans Shank, Hans Brubaker, Henry Musselman, with their families embracing 363 persons came to Philadelphia a few days before September 8, 1717, where they seem to have been met by Martin Kendig and Hans Herr who conducted them to Lancaster Co, PA (This information was taken from the "Origin of the Kneisley Family" history book). Supposedly funds for the voyage where supplied by Queen

Ann, the Queen of England. This passage was arraigned by the Mennonites who had come to America in 1710 and managed to convince the Queen that these Mennonites would make good patriots for the Queen in British America.

Following is some information on a journey across the ocean that was recorded in a journal by an Amish passenger, who traveled on the ship Charming Nancy in 1737. The ship our family traveled on was likely to have been smaller than the ship in this 1737 article, so conditions may have been worse.

This information was taken from "Miscellaneous Amish Mennonite Documents," Pennsylvania Mennonite Heritage 2 (July 1979): 12.

"The 28th of June while in Rotterdam (in the Netherlands) getting ready to start my Zernbli died and was buried in Rotterdam. The 29th we got under sail and enjoyed one and a half days of favorable wind. The 7th day of July, early in the morning, Hans Zimmerman's son-in-law died. "

"We landed in England the 8th of July, remaining 9 days in port during which 5 children died. Several days before Michael's Georgli had died."

"On the 29th of July three children died. On the first of August my Hansli died and the Tuesday previous 5 children died. On the 3rd of August contrary winds beset the vessel and from the first to the 7th of the month three more children died. On the 8th of August, Shambien's Lizzie died and on the 9th Hans Zimmerman's Jacobli died. On the 19th, Christian Burgli's child died. Passed a ship on the 21st. A favorable wind sprang up. On the 28th Hans Gasi's wife died. Passed a ship 13th of September."

Landed in Philadelphia on the 18th and my wife and I left ship on the 19th. A child was born to us on the 20th – died – wife recovered. A voyage of 83 days."

Following is another article on a larger immigrant ship explaining the difficulty of the journey.

The following article was taken from the book "Immigrant Ships" by Paul A. Darrel.

"Many sailing vessels made annual runs from England to the colonies. Other vessels made the crossing only once. None of these vessels was very large. The ship (and therefore three-masted) Patience made annual runs to Philadelphia from 1748 to 1753, with the exception of 1752 when she arrived at Annapolis. Klaus Wurst has given particulars: the Patience was a 200-ton ship, had 8 guns, and a crew of 16. In 1748, the Patience carried 122 men over 16 (total passengers not given); in 1749, 137 men, 270 persons; in 1750, 124 men, 266 persons; in 1751, 255 persons; in 1752, 260 persons; in 1753, 108 persons.

Immigrant passengers were densely packed, with little space, often with poor food and bad water. Under such conditions, disease was commonplace. Some captains were considerate and kept to the terms of the contract, but not all. It is worth noting that the total passengers on the Royal Enterprise (1750) were given as 'souls'; more often, passengers were listed as 'Palatines' or 'Foreigners', but sometimes as, 'Freights', as if they were mere cargo.

Upon arrival at Philadelphia, males over the age of 16 were taken to the City Hall for the oath of allegiance, then led back to the ship. Those who had their passage money, or could borrow it, were released. The others were consigned to merchants, and announcements were printed in newspapers. Buyers bargained with the passengers for a stated period of service, and paid the merchant the passage money and any other debts. Families were often divided on arrival, as children were 'sold' to pay the family's passage.

Passengers who were sick were not allowed to land. If there was infectious disease on board, the ship had to remove one mile from the port. In 1743, the Assembly at Philadelphia purchased Fisher Island, later named Province Island, its buildings to be used as a hospital. In 1754, 253 persons died there, as recorded in the accounts of one undertaker. The merchants to whom the passengers had been consigned assumed burial expenses."

These ships became known as coffin ships, due to the method of storing the passengers in boxes with an open end. The passengers were frequently called and recorded in ship manifests as cargo. They were slid into these boxes from an open end and remained confined in these boxes for long periods of time. They were permitted to leave their boxes in small groups to walk around the bottom of the hold, but were normally not allowed to go up on the deck. It was a very difficult and hazardous journey for all that made the trip. Our ancestors made a great sacrifice to bring our family to this new country. It took pioneer spirit and great courage to make this journey, a courage that would be tested again in the years that followed.

The Kneisle's in Lancaster

They were taken to Lancaster after landing in Philadelphia. The group of Mennonites, who came to the area in 1710, had established a small community in that area. Each of the new arriving families was given a grant of land from William Penn and the necessary tools to begin farming the land. Antonius was given land about one mile west of Lancaster where the Harrisburg Pike ran across his property and the Swarr Run also ran through his property. Antonius and his son Hans eventually built and operated a water wheel grinding mill on the Swarr Run. The entire community would have pitched in to help them build their houses and barns, much as you see at barn raisings today in the Amish and Mennonite communities. The community grew by leaps and bounds as more and more Mennonites moved from Europe to the Lancaster area. Families began to grow and land was starting to become crowded. By 1729, Lancaster County was established and in 1730 the town of Lancaster was named the county seat. In 1729, due to the large number of people living in the area, a large purchase of land was made in Massanuttin (now Page County), Virginia by Abraham Strickler. A large number of the Kneisley family members migrated to that area and began to raise families there. At least four of Antonius's children moved to the Shenandoah Valley in Virginia to farm and raise their families. This would be about the time Adam Sr. was born and would indicate there was a shortage of property for farming and may have led to Adam Sr. becoming a wagon driver as he grew older.

It was probably due to the crowded conditions in Lancaster that would make someone want to leave a growing community like Lancaster and head out into the wild frontier. However since he was the last child of Antonius, he most likely would not have received any land at Antonius's passing. We believe Adam Sr. was employed by the British during the French and Indian War, as a Conestoga wagon driver, delivering goods and supplies to the Fort at Ligonier and at Fort Pitt. Records from the French and Indian War indicate that many of the soldiers and support personnel returned to Philadelphia with information on the location of land along the Forbes Road that they wanted to move to and obtained a land grant from Ben Franklin. We believe Adam Sr. received his grant from General Arthur St Clair since his property was adjacent to the General's property. It was reported that St Clair gave grants of property, adjacent to his land; to people he felt would make good neighbors. Adam Sr. was granted 1,200 acres of land in Southwestern Pennsylvania, about 4 miles west of the site of the newly constructed Fort Ligonier along the Forbes Road, that bordered St Clair's property. Adam Sr. would have most likely traveled along this property, that bordered the Forbes trail, while carrying supplies to Fort Pitt. So with his wife and other family members he proceeded to move to his new homestead circa 1761. During that same year their first son Anthony was born in Westmoreland County. Adam Sr. and his wife probably traveled on this journey with some other relatives and friends. The most likely of these would have been his half brother George Eager and his half sister Anna Marie Eager, who was married to George Keltz and his mother Elizabeth Yeager, who was probably with them since Adam Sr., George and Anna Marie were her children. We have never found any indication of her burial in the Ligonier area, but grave markers from that time period deteriorated quickly. The Forbes Road, in this time period, was a fairly active road with Conestoga wagons traveling in both directions, carrying goods and essential needs for the British troops stationed at the forts along the way making it a heavily traveled supply road for the west. The courage to make this trip, to a new and dangerous land, was probably driven by Adam Sr.'s desire to become a landowner. It makes one wonder if Adam Sr. and Elizabeth had any idea of the danger that awaited them in the Ligonier Valley.

CHAPTER TWO

The Ligonier Valley

In 1717, at the time the Kneisle's were arriving in America, Ligonier was the wild frontier and was occupied mainly by American Indians. Ligonier was located in a beautiful valley surrounded by mountains in all directions in Southwestern Pennsylvania. It lay west of the Laurel Hill and east of the Chestnut Ridge. In the early 1700's, this area was known as Loyalhanning, named for an Indian village settled by the Delaware Indians after their departure from the Susquehanna area around 1727. The village was located along the Loyalhanna Creek about a mile east of the current reconstructed Fort Ligonier. The name Loyalhanning refers to "middle stream" since the stream was located near the middle of the major rivers located to the north, east, south, and west of it. Later on, the middle stream became known by its current name, the Loyalhanna Creek. There were some trappers and traders dealing with the Indians in this area during the 1740's, but very few settlers.

In the 1750's, both the British and the French laid claim to the land west of the Allegheny Mountains. The French wanted to control the Ohio and Mississippi Rivers so they could ship their furs from the interior to New Orleans, Detroit, and the Canadian colonies. The Ohio River, at that time including the section that is now called the Allegheny River, wound north towards the Canadian border. The British were upset that they were being restricted to the valuable lands and goods west of the Ohio. The early Pennsylvania traders and settlers who were living along the Ohio River found themselves caught in the middle of the French from the north and the Virginians from the south, with both groups fighting to gain control over this area. It was only a matter of time until war would begin over this section of America. In 1752, the Ottawa Indians, who were pro-French, destroyed the trading post at Pickawillany, which later became known as Piqua, Ohio. The following year the French built a series of forts from north to south, including a fort named Fort Duquesne at the forks of the Ohio and the Monongahela, the future location of Pittsburgh, Pennsylvania. These forts were built to strengthen the French claim to the land west and north of the Ohio River. The storm clouds of war were now forming.

The Virginians and the British in 1755, led by Major General Edward Braddock, constructed a road north from Virginia that would be used to attack Fort Duquesne. The British efforts to attack the fort from this route failed. The route was plagued by many problems including the difficulty of crossing the Monongahela River before reaching Fort Duquesne. Colonel Henry Bouquet, under the command of General John Forbes, in 1758, began building a new road from Philadelphia to the west. This new road was seen as a better route to mount an attack on the French and Indians at Fort Duquesne. This new route would avoid the need to cross the Monongahela River in order to attack Fort Duquesne. When Bouquet reached Loyalhanning, he constructed a fort along the northern bank of the Loyalhanning on the crest of a hill overlooking the middle stream. The objective was to set up a supply depot for the 5,000 British troops needed to attack Fort Duquesne. The place he selected was an ideal location. It was located approximately 50 miles east of Fort Duquesne, which would supply a good staging location for his attack. On the south of the land, he chose, was a rocky bluff or perpendicular rocky wall between the fort and the Loyalhanna Creek. This was a natural barrier against attack from the south. The fort rose to ninety-four feet above the water of the creek. On the north was a deep ravine that was a natural barrier. General John Forbes named the fort, Fort Ligonier, in honor of Sir John Ligonier, Commander-in-Chief of the British Armies. Fort Ligonier, established in 1758, was the last in a string of Forts built along the Forbes Road in support of the British attack on Fort Duquesne. The fort was completed in September 1758 and the British troops quickly made an attack on Fort Duquesne on September 14th, which was repelled by a very strong French and Indian force. After that initial battle, the French and Indians set out to attack the supply fort and drive the British out of the area. The fort at Ligonier withstood the strong counter-attack by the French and Indians on October 12, 1758 and due to the large number of British soldiers, about 4,000 strong, now stationed at Fort Ligonier, the French quickly retreated back to Fort Duquesne. With the onset of winter approaching Forbes decided that it was not the right time to attack Fort Duquesne. However, in November, Forbes received word that the French were abandoning Fort Duquesne and so he quickly organized his soldiers and headed out to capture Fort Duquesne. On November 25th, Forbes took possession of Fort Duquesne without a battle and named the site, Pittsburg, in honor of the Secretary of State William Pitt. Later in the 1800's an "h" was added and the name became Pittsburgh.

During the next eight years, Fort Ligonier served as a link in the supply line for the new Fort Pitt and points to the west. During Pontiac's War of 1763, Native American Indians from the Seneca tribe attacked the fort on two different occasions, but on both occasions the soldiers at the fort successfully repelled the invaders. In 1766, the fort was decommissioned from active service, having never been overtaken by enemy forces. It fell into disrepair and was not rebuilt until the restoration started in the 1950's. Around

1774, a small fort was built on the banks of the Loyalhanna to provide protection due to the Indian raids in and around the town of Ligonier. This fort was named Fort Preservation. The exact location of this fort is not known.

The Enemy in the Forests and the Hills

During the period of time from 1758 until 1790, there was constant danger in the area outside the Fort and throughout the Ligonier Valley from the American Indians. This area was suffering from constant wars and battles. The American Indians were losing their land to the French and English and were under constant movement to the west. The Indians would establish treaties with the different countries only to see the treaties broken. The Indians were in constant defense of their lands and were fighting with the English to prevent losing more land. The land west of the Allegheny Mountain was to remain in control of the Indians, but the settlers just kept coming and moving further west. The Indians rose up in arms to protect their land and to stop this westward flow of settlers. It was literally a war zone and a difficult and hazardous place for both the settlers and the American Indians.

In the middle 1770's, renegade whites began to join up with the Indians. The renegade whites were more dangerous for the settlers than the Indians, but both groups caused serious life threatening problems for the settlers who had been living there and for the new arrivals trying to set up homesteads. During the French and Indian War, the Indians were divided with some fighting for the British and others fighting for the French. In 1763, The Treaty of Paris ended the French and Indian War. The French began to pull out of the land west of the Ohio River. The Indians feared that without the support of the French, the settlers would continue to move westward on to their land. Chief Pontiac got the tribes to band together to attack the settlers and the British forts that had been built in the area. Pontiac's War lasted only until 1764, but it was 1766 before Chief Pontiac officially surrendered to the British. The Proclamation of 1763, signed by King George III of England, prohibited any English settlement west of the Appalachian mountains and required those already settled in those regions to return east in an attempt to ease tensions with Native Americans. However, this caused problems with the British Colonists and the Frontier settlers and discontent with British rule begins to develop. During the period of time from 1766 until 1775, there were sporadic Indian raids into the area around Ligonier Valley mostly due to the Indian's dissatisfaction with the settlers living in the area west of the Allegheny's. The settlers from the central Appalachian Mountains attempted to establish a new colony stretching from Western Pennsylvania south through what is now West Virginia and into the western part of Virginia. They felt they were too far removed from the safety and protection of the British armies and felt the need to set up their own Province and to provide their own protection. They petitioned the Continental Congress in Philadelphia in 1775 requesting permission to establish a 14th colony that would be named the Province and Government of Westsylvania. The petition was stalled in committee. In 1776, the Westsylvanian's allowed their petition to die, so that the United States of America could be established. It was during this period of time that the colonists became more disenchanted with British rule and began to test the British control of the Colonies.

When the American Revolution began, in October 1775 the Colonists met with the Shawnee, Mingo, and Delaware Indian Tribal leaders and struck an agreement to settle their differences. This resulted with the Indian leaders agreeing to remain neutral in the Colonist's conflict with Great Britain, but many of the other Native Indian Tribes, Shawnee, Delaware and the Iroquois, near the Great Lakes, allied with the British. The Indians could see the continued westward movement of the settlers. It appeared that the Indians felt the British were a better alternative than the Colonists for keeping their land free from the settlers. The Indian's main purpose was to discourage the settlers from moving farther west onto Indian lands and to drive them back east. The British used the Indians to strike at the Colonies from the west. The British at Fort Detroit under Colonel Henry Hamilton supplied the war parties and often led the Indian warriors in the battles against the settlers. Colonel Hamilton earned the name of "Hair Buyer" by the Indians from the payments he made for American scalps. The British officers also bought captives from the Indians and used them as servants both in America and in England.

The renegade whites also allied themselves with the Indians during this period of time and became leaders that were more brutal than most of the Indian tribes. These men had left civilization behind, joined various Indian tribes, and adopted the Indian mode of life and warfare. In some cases these men were deserters from the American Army who went over to the English, or, perhaps, to the Indians. It may have been due to the alluring rewards offered on the part of British officers for scalps. These men were more dangerous to the settlers than the Indians, because they knew the weak points of the settlement, knew the territory, and knew more about the individual bravery or weakness of the individual settlers. Attacks led by these white renegades were more brutal and bloodthirsty than any attack by the Indians. These outlaws were responsible for a lot of the attacks and problems brought down on the residents of Westmoreland County.

In 1774, Arthur St. Clair, recognizing a need to protect the settlers in the area, organized the Frontier Rangers in the Ligonier Valley area. There was a proclamation issued encouraging young men to turn out to fight the Indians in small parties, and in a manner resembling the Indian style of fighting. This was very attractive to small parties of energetic young men. These groups were called "Rangers". These were all bold young men who went out dressed in homemade clothing, each armed at his own expense, and comparatively well armed for that day, each carrying a rifle or a musket, a knife, and a hatchet. They acted together, or separately, as the occasion demanded. They stood together for protection, and were frequently neighbors and friends who would not stop at any danger to rescue a neighbor or friend from a difficult situation. They had officers whom they obeyed, whether they were in small parties or engaged in a general turnout for public defense. These men were at home in the woods, and upon any sign of danger they knew how to travel by the shortest route to the place of need. They would spread the news of the presence of attacking Indians over an entire community, and very rapidly gather the women and children to the nearest blockhouse or place of safety. Having spent many years in the woods they could travel through the forest on dark nights with confidence. Their hearing and sight were sharpened by constant use so that even the slightest movement in the bushes was noticed by them, and sounds which others could not hear were distinctly heard and understood by them. They could endure long tramps through the woods and over mountains, without food. They were rapid runners and experts in the use of a rifle and were excellent marksmen, whether moving or standing. All these qualities came from the need to be alert as they were traveling around the area alert for Indian attacks and required for their own self-preservation. During these early years, these skills were the salvation of the pioneers. The women of this time were no less heroic, tested under the same circumstances as the men and in many cases had to fight to protect their young and their homesteads, while the men were working in the fields away from the house.

The settlers in the area of Four-Mile Run, near the original Kneisle homestead, had built a strong blockhouse on land owned by a farmer named Richard Williams that became known as Fort Williams. Richard Williams was the Captain of a company of Frontier Rangers. Adam Kneisle Sr. and his brother in law and neighbor George Keltz were privates in Captain Williams' company and Adam Sr.'s half brother George Eager, also a neighbor, was a Captain. The settlers from both Indian Creek and Four-Mile Run had access to this blockhouse. It was located on the western side of the main road leading from Ligonier to Donegal. The settlers of the area gathered here in times of danger, since they were too far from Ligonier to go to the new fort, Fort Preservation, located there. The blowing of a horn, which could be heard for up to two miles echoing off the hills, was used as a method of alerting the settlers in the area that danger was imminent. The horn would bring armed Frontier Rangers to the area of the alert and the settlers and their families would move as quickly as possible to the blockhouse. If a strong attack seemed imminent, a fast rider would be sent off alerting other companies of Rangers in the Ligonier Valley to assist in the battles and warning other settlers to move to their respective blockhouses. In some cases the sounding of the horn would scare away the renegades or Indians, if they were only a small raiding party. These blockhouses were strongly constructed log buildings that could hold up to three dozen settlers. Space was very limited when there were three dozen settlers inside. The size of the blockhouse on the outside was approximately 20 by 21 feet. The blockhouse had heavy doors and heavy window protection, which could be put up and barred, from the inside. There were holes in the outer log walls through which rifles could be aimed and shot to protect the settlers inside. There were gaps and cracks near the gables of the building to let in light and air. There was usually an upper level inside the building, which was a platform around the outer walls, where settlers could stand or lay to aim and shoot through openings, with their rifles, down on the surrounding area. There was also a fireplace that could be used to heat the blockhouse and to prepare meals. The blockhouses were built in the middle of a clearing, so it was difficult for anyone to sneak up on it. Indians approaching them took their lives in their own hands. Because of their construction, a group of settlers with a few flintlock rifles could hold off groups of attackers much larger in number than the group of settlers. They could withstand long sieges, since they were normally well stocked with ammunition and food by the settlers. Once the Indians had satisfied themselves and left the area the settlers gathered up their belongings and their scattered live stock and moved back to their log houses. In periods of constant danger, the settler's families would remain in and around the blockhouse during the day and the men would move to the farms in large groups to care for their crops and livestock. They would rotate from farm to farm so that each farm received some attention on a regular basis.

Colonel Archibald Lockry commanded a company of Frontier Rangers near Latrobe. He had a blockhouse constructed on a property near the present site of St. Vincent College.

In November of 1777, Lockry wrote in a letter.

"on the north side of Forbes Road, the people are kept in the forts and cannot get subsistence from their plantations. They made application requesting us to put them under pay or receive rations. We are obligated to adopt them, as we have no other means to stop them from leaving the county. Eleven persons were killed at Fort Palmer near Ligonier and the Indians left a proclamation from General Hamilton in Detroit, requesting all persons to come to him to receive payment, lodgings, and 200 acres of land. I have ventured to erect two stockades at Ligonier and Hannastown as places of refuge. "

Colonel Archibald Lockry and Captain Richard Williams were listed as beloved friends in George Keltz's will. As a result there is a high probability that the restored blockhouse near Latrobe, PA was very similar to the blockhouse that was located near Four-Mile Run and was probably one of the two mentioned in his letter. The blockhouse near Latrobe was found inside an older house several years ago and has undergone a reconstruction with many of the original logs still intact. Following are some pictures of the exterior and interior of the restored Lockry blockhouse, located near St. Vincent College, north of Route 30, near Latrobe.

Exterior Front View

Front View of the Restored Lockry Blockhouse

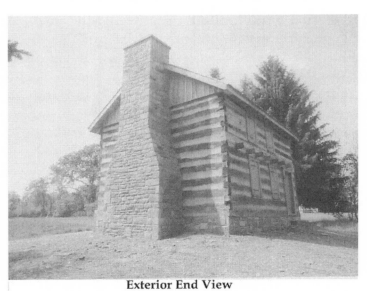

Exterior End View

End View of the Restored Lockry Blockhouse

Second Story

Interior View of the Restored Lockry Blockhouse

Interior Fireplace

Interior View of the Restored Lockry Blockhouse

It was into this chaos and turmoil that Adam Kneisle Sr. moved his family, far from the safety of the Lancaster area. The pioneer spirit and courage of the Kneisle family continued to be evident in their character during this period of time.

The Kneisle Family Moves to Ligonier

The Kneisle's stayed in the Lancaster area until circa 1761, when Adam Sr. made the decision to move to his land grant in the Ligonier Valley. Family history indicates that they walked from Lancaster to their new homestead, a journey of over 210 miles. It would have taken about three weeks to make this journey. They probably had Adam Sr.'s Conestoga wagon loaded with their possessions and perhaps a few farm animals to start their farm in the valley.

The Westmoreland County History book indicates that Anthony and his brothers Jacob and John made the trip to Ligonier. This information is not correct, since it was Adam Sr. who obtained the Land Grant. My Grandfather Charles Edward Nicely always talked about Adam Kneisle (Nicely) and the Adam Kneisle (Nicely) farm near Four-Mile Run and to the members of our family that seemed to indicate Adam Sr. was the pioneer who settled in the Ligonier Valley. Westmoreland County records indicate a patent, the final deed from the Commonwealth, was issued to Adam Nicely Sr. with no mention of Anthony Nicely.

The typical Mennonite farmer, in the mid 1700's, typically had many acres of ground he could call his own, separated by as much as a mile or more from his nearest neighbors. They normally settled down where they found a river, a spring or a grove that pleased them. Adam Sr. and Elizabeth's farm followed this same pattern. Their homestead was located a little over 4 miles southwest of Fort Ligonier about a half a mile above the western side of the Four-Mile Run on the western most section of their land grant. They choose a piece of land situated about halfway up the eastern side of the Chestnut Ridge. The ground in the area they chose to farm was fairly level with a gently rising slope to the west toward the Chestnut Ridge and to the east sloping down to the Four-Mile Run. In the forest they went about constructing dwellings of logs, clearing a large part of their acreage and beginning to plant corn and other crops.

Since they were separated from their neighbors by such large distances made it difficult to protect themselves from the Indian attacks that were occurring throughout the area. The Westmoreland County History Book indicates that they suffered frequently and severely from the aggressions of the Indians. The History book also indicates that a Jacob Kneisle lost a wife and two children, who were killed by the Indians, and it so discouraged him that he moved from the Ligonier Valley area to Armstrong County in Pennsylvania. The History Book reported that many Nicely's in Armstrong County claim a Jacob Nicely as their ancestor. I have never been able to find anything to support this section of the Westmoreland History book. I am also unable to find any support for the report, in the Westmoreland History Book that a John Kneisle also settled in this area. All of the descendants I have located were descendants of Adam and Elizabeth Eichert Kneisle (Nicely) Sr. and I cannot find any indication of a land patent in the name of Jacob Kneisle (Nicely). In spite of all of the strife going on in the area, Adam and Elizabeth Kneisle Sr.'s family continued to grow, increasing in number as they struggled to establish their farm and live their lives, while keeping their family safe from harm.

CHAPTER THREE

Adam Kneisle Sr.'s Family

Adam and Elizabeth Eichert Kneisle Sr. lived on their land during very difficult times from 1761 until 1790. In addition to the constant danger of Indian attacks, it was a difficult life just to get established. The early settlers to this area brought with their family a very scanty supply of this world's goods. In many cases they often had little more than a rifle, an ax and a mattock. Some of the settlers stayed at Fort Ligonier in the early 1760's and walked to their farms during the day to establish their homesteads. Other settlers moved onto their land and lived in huts or lean-tos built against a rock or a bank and covered with bark. Building near a spring or small stream was also a high priority. Once they were settled, they began to clear away the trees to establish an area where their crops might grow.

It is difficult to understand and appreciate the hardships these people faced and endured. Their early farms were called "deadenings" or "clearings. The term "deadening" refers to the practice of cutting a ring around the trunk of a tree near the ground, deep enough to stop the sap from supplying the tree. The trees cut in this manner died, killing the leaves allowing the farmers to plant their crops between the trees, enabling the sun light to reach the crops aiding in their growth. The term "clearing" refers to the opening that was made once all the trees had been cut down and the stumps removed from the area. Theses early settlers could not transport grain from the east for bread, in fact they were happy to get enough for seed. Out of necessity they had to live on the meager products of a new garden, wild berry, and on game, which was abundant in the woods. They were relatively safe in the early days, since one man or a small family could live unnoticed and unmolested by the Indians. However, once the numbers of settlers increased, it increased the possibility of being seen and attacked by the Indians. It was a continuous warfare for life against the wild and unforgiving soil, as well as against the Indians.

During the first year on the homestead, the log house had to be constructed, which meant cutting down and shaping the logs for the house as well as for the barn. A typical single floor log home required 20 to 30 large logs and a variety of smaller logs, plus slabs for the roof and a supply of mud to fill the gaps between the logs. The logs from the clearing operation would have been used when possible. The house had to be fortified with heavy doors and window covers that could be put in place to protect the family during an Indian attack. They also had to begin farming at least enough to support themselves and their animals. Everything they needed to establish their homestead had to be manufactured: Furniture, household items, clothing, and other goods necessary for use in the home and on the farm. They would need to be self-sufficient, since they were located a long distance from their closest neighbors. There were some supplies and staples that could be purchased from the troops at Fort Ligonier, but that was over an hour ride into Ligonier to purchase the supplies.

Despite these hardships the Kneisle's established their home and developed the land to support their family and their livestock. There would have been fruit trees in the area around the Kneisle log house in typical German farming tradition. There would have been water close by. In this case there is a spring about 30 feet away from where the home once stood. The barn would be located close to the house. In spite of all this activity, the Kneisle family continued to grow. Their oldest son Anthony was born circa 1761 being born just after they moved to the Ligonier area. Their oldest daughter Rosanna was brought into the family circa 1764. Their next child was Adam Jr., who was born circa 1765. Their fourth child was a daughter Mary Elizabeth, born in 1765, followed by another daughter Catherine circa 1766. Their sixth child was a boy named Jacob. He was born on May 22, 1770. The roving teacher, Balthaser Meyer, baptized Jacob on November 16, 1772. This baptism was recorded in the records of the Harolds Lutheran Church. His Godparents were George and Anna Maria Eager Keltz. As mentioned earlier, George and Adam Sr. were brother in laws and their farms were located relatively close to each other. In 1774, both Adam Sr. and George would serve as privates with the Company of Frontier Rangers under the command of Captain Richard Williams.

The Capture of Jacob

In the early summer of 1775, the American Revolutionary War was developing into an all out battle against the British. Indian raids into the Ligonier Valley were increasing as a result of the British alliance with the Indians. In the meantime the Kneisle family was going about the normal daily chores of farming and living off the land. On a fateful day in late July of 1775 Anthony, the oldest son at 14 years of age, was most likely working on the farm with his father. Elizabeth, the mother, was working in the home baking. The other five children Rosanna, age 12, Adam Jr., age 11, Mary Elizabeth, age 10, Catherine, age 9, and Jacob, age 5, were most likely the children who had been sent a short distance away from the house to pick blackberries. After a short time of picking, Jacob went back to the house, where his mother was baking, and she gave him a cake to take out to share with the other children. The cake was hot and part way to the berry patch, Jacob returned to the house because it was too hot to carry. His mother cooled down the cake and he headed out once again for the berry patch. About halfway back to the berry patch a small band of Indians, who had been hiding in the woods, were watching Jacob's movements and came out of the woods and captured Jacob. The other children heard him yelling and could see the Indians carrying him away. The Indians with Jacob in hand headed down the hill through the woods towards the Four-Mile Run, located about a half mile east of the farm. The children ran to the home and alerted their mother as to what had happened. They also ran to tell their father Adam Sr. and their brother Anthony. Adam Sr. quickly gathered some friends and neighbors and took off in pursuit of the Indians. The process of gathering help was probably accomplished by blowing the alert horn, which would have brought a group of Frontier Rangers to the site of the horn blower. Since Adam Sr. was a member of the Frontier Rangers, it is likely that the members of the search were Frontier Rangers who served with Adam Sr. Once the search party was assembled at the Kneisle farm, they took off in pursuit of the Indians and Jacob.

The Indians, carrying Jacob, about a half a mile below the farm, began to follow the Four-Mile Run in a northerly direction traveling about two and one half miles to the junction with the Loyalhanna Creek. They then began to follow the Loyalhanna Creek westward towards what is today the town of Latrobe and then continued to follow the creek north to Saltsburg. Near Saltsburg, the Loyalhanna flows into the Kiskiminetas River. Adam Sr.'s search party was able to track them through the woods and along the streams all the way to the Kiskiminetas River. However, when they reached the Kiskiminetas River, they lost the trail in the forest and had to return home without Jacob. In 1775, the land north of the Kiskiminetas River was Indian country and was a dense wilderness.

The story of Jacob's capture became widespread in the Ligonier Valley and many people of the Valley knew the story. It would be 50 years before the Kneisle family would find out that Jacob had survived following that very sad and heartbreaking day. During the ensuing years, Jacob's mother and father and their families began a long period of mourning and sadness not knowing what had or would become of their young son and relative. It was said that Adam Sr. could not discuss Jakey without tears coming to his eyes. Adam Sr. passed away in 1826 shortly after finding out that his son Jacob lived and had raised a family.

The Family Lives on Without Jacob

The family continued to grow after Jacob was captured. A daughter Margaret was born on June 10, 1784. Then on October 29, 1786, the last child, a daughter Ann Elizabeth was born. The original log home served as a birthplace for all these children and for several generations to come. During this period of time Indian raids continued into the area with many settlers and members of the settlers families killed or captured. One can only wonder what went through the minds of Adam Sr. and his friends as they fought their battles with the Indians. There was probably a great deal of anger towards the attacking Indians as a result of the capture of Adam Sr.'s son Jacob.

The Kneisle family continued to improve the farm in the Mennonite tradition of crop rotation, which over the years would enrich the soil and produce excellent crops. The Kneisle family was credited in the Westmoreland History Book with setting the standard for this farming technique that spread through the Ligonier Valley. Jacob's brother Anthony stayed on at the original homestead living in the original log house and developing the land. His brother Adam Jr., circa

1799, moved to the other end of the 1200 acres and set up his own homestead. When Adam Sr. died in 1826, each of the two sons was willed 600 acres of the original land grant. Anthony married the widow Sarah Salome Hargnett Herr circa 1806. Sarah had five children to her first husband John Herr and these children came to live with Anthony. John Herr may have been a descendant of Hans Herr, who was in the first group of Mennonites who came to America in 1710. Anthony continued to work on the farm clearing over 200 acres for planting. In 1810, he constructed and moved into a new home on the original homestead, which is still standing today. Anthony and Sarah's first child named Anthony Wayne was born in the original log house on August 2, 1807. Their second and third children were twins and were the last of the children born in the original log house. George and Eliza May were born on March 21, 1810. The next child was a daughter Elizabeth born on March 5, 1811 soon followed by a son named Adam IV on November 25, 1812. The last two children according to family history were born in the new home built by Anthony. Between 1810 and 1830 the name had changed from Kneisle to the current spelling of Nicely as it appeared in the 1830 Census. Anthony erected a new barn and several outbuildings, raised good stock and in all respects greatly improved the place. In politics, Anthony was a Whig (Republican) and it is said of him that he never missed an election. They were members of the Lutheran church.

Jacob's sister Rosanna was married to William Kerns circa 1784. They had a son Adam who married a Catherine, but there is no further information available at this time.

Jacob's brother Adam Jr. made his homestead about two miles south of Ligonier along the Ligonier to Donegal road circa 1799. The barn at that location carried a sign showing a date of 1800 for many years. The homestead is located west of Route 711, about a mile across the road from the Ligonier Country Club course. The house standing there today still has the original log house inside of the current structure. He also developed his farm and homestead. He married a Mary or Sarah, not sure which name is correct, whose maiden name we have not been able to find, circa 1799. They had eight children, Margaret in 1800, Adam III circa 1801, Elizabeth circa 1802, John Fuller on May 3, 1803, Rosanna circa 1804, George A. on May 11, 1805, Jacob circa 1809, and Martha circa 1810. Mary or Sarah passed away after 1810 and Adam Jr. took a second wife, Esther Shirey, sometime after Mary or Sarah's death and prior to 1822. There is a Mary Nicely buried in the Keltz Cemetery who was born on February 22, 1778 and died on August 1, 1819. She is the right age to be Adam Jr.'s first wife and the death date agrees with his marriage to Esther Shirey and would seem to indicate his first wife was Mary. Esther and Adam Jr. would have seven children. Two children were born prior to 1825, the year in which Jacob was found in Ohio, Catherine on June 10, 1821, and Susanna in 1822, The other five children were born after Jacob was found, Anthony A. on June 26, 1827, Philip and David, twins were born on April 9, 1830, Louisa on August 19, 1832, William July 24, 1834 and Henry June 23, 1837. Adam Jr. was also a farmer and developed his farm into a very prosperous operation.

Jacob's sister Catherine married John Piper circa 1786 and while I do not have any record of their family, there are many Pipers in the Ligonier Valley area, These Pipers were most likely relatives of the John Piper who married Catherine.

Jacob's sister Mary Elizabeth married Joseph Keruens and I cannot locate any information on their family.

Jacob's sister Margaret married George Ambrose circa 1803. George and Margaret had seven children and lived somewhere in the area near where her brother Adam Jr. had established his homestead. Their farm was called "Freedom", so named by George's father John Fredrick Ambrose from whom he inherited the land. The land was located in the area west of Ligonier on the road to Stahlstown, somewhere near the Adam Nicely Jr. farm. Their children were Margaret, born on December 20, 1804, Fredrick, born circa 1805, Elizabeth, born circa 1806, Mary, born September 14, 1810, Catherine, born circa 1814, Louise, born on August 5, 1817, and Sarah, born on April 29, 1821.

Jacob's sister Ann Elizabeth married Michael Miller circa 1806, but to date I do not have any information on their family.

The family grew and prospered in the years after Jacob was captured. However, in 1825, the whole family was in for an unexpected surprise. They were about to find out what happened to Jacob following his capture by the Indians.

Finding Jacob Kneisle

In 1825, a trader, John Wolfe, from the Ligonier Valley who knew the Nicely family, was trading with the Seneca Indians in Ohio and came in contact with a white man dressed as an Indian. He was familiar with the story concerning the capture of Jacob Kneisle and he thought the man resembled the men in the Kneisle family. He talked with the man and found out that it was Jacob, who was now living as an Indian. The trader returned to Ligonier Valley and informed Jacob's father and mother about what he had found. His father Adam Sr. was 95 and his mother Elizabeth was 90 years old. She had been repeating for years that she would not be able to go to her grave in peace not knowing what had happened to her son Jakey. The parents requested that one of their sons go and meet with Jacob and ask him to return to see her. We are not sure which son went to meet with Jacob. However, an Ohio newspaper report talked about Jacob's father coming to see

Jacob and since his father's name was Adam, we feel it was Adam Jr. son of Adam Sr. that actually made the trip. Adam Jr. would have been 61 years old at the time.

Traveling on horseback, he made the trip to the Seneca tribe and found Jacob. They recognized each other and had a good visit. Jacob had been adopted into the Seneca Indian nation, was living as an Indian with a family, was prosperous and had accumulated land and many possessions. Jacob did not want to return with his brother, but had promised that he would return next year to visit with his mother. Jacob did return partway with his brother, on the trip back, giving him a rifle and other farm tools as gifts and each continued on his own to his respective homes. However, Jacob never did fulfill his promise to come back to see his mother. The family thought that Jacob might have died before he could fulfill his promise. His father died in 1826 and his mother passed away circa 1829, never seeing her son Jacob again, but at least she knew he had lived through his capture. While she was probably disappointed that he did not return to see her, it was probably a comfort to her, in her final years, knowing he had been found and was alive. A story that was passed down, in the family, indicated that when Jacob was a young man he had made a journey back to Westmoreland County in an effort to find his family. Since he could not remember the area and could not pronounce the family name, he returned to his Indian family and the tribe.

The visit in 1825 was the last the family heard from Jacob. For the next 178 years, the story was passed down from generation to generation. It was known that he had a wife and children, but we had either not been told or it was forgotten that he was called Tsu-Ka-We or Crow and that he was found in Ohio. In any case, we had no information with which we could begin to track down him or his descendents. We knew he was with the Seneca Indians, but no indication was passed down regarding where the Seneca tribe was located. We knew that the Seneca's were in New York State, but records also indicated they were spread out into Ohio. There was a mention of a Warren but we couldn't determine if it was Warren, a town, or Warren, a county and Ohio and Pennsylvania both have a town and a county named Warren. So the mystery continued into Calendar 2003.

There are now over nine generations of the Adam and Elizabeth Eichert Nicely Sr.'s family that have been born and raised in the Ligonier Valley and the family has spread to all parts of the United States. However, there was always some emptiness and sadness in the hearts of the descendents of the Nicely family not knowing what happened to Jacob Kneisle and his family following the meeting in 1825. However, through a very strange set of circumstances the mystery was about to be solved and uncovered in Calendar 2003.

CHAPTER FOUR

The Whitecrow Family Search

Traditionally, tribal culture, language and history are preserved and passed down to other generations by tribal elders and families through stories and legends told to the young, and through ceremonial songs and dances. The knowledge that the Whitecrow family had descended from a captured boy named Jacob Knisely, whose Indian name was Crow or Tsu-ka-we, was passed down as older members told their children of family relationships and life events. The information on eight generations of ancestors back to Crow was obtained from the memories of current living descendents which led to the location of two written accountings of the capture and subsequent visit by Jacob's brother. Those descendents of Crow, or Tsu-ka-we, currently living also have memories of Grandpa Alfred Whitecrow, great grandson of Jacob or Crow, and Chief of the Seneca-Cayuga Tribe at the time of his death in 1932, and his wife, Mary Spicer Whitecrow, mentioning this fact as they raised their family.

Virginia Scritchfield Wood, a granddaughter of Alfred and Mary Whitecrow, served as Secretary of the tribe for several years and had been very active in the research and preservation of the history of the Whitecrow family and Seneca-Cayuga Tribe. In 1974, Mayo Sidney "Sid" Whitecrow, Jr., a grandson of Alfred and Mary Whitecrow, was hired as the first Business Manager of the Seneca-Cayuga Tribe of Oklahoma, establishing the tribal office, implementing programs, and creating economic development which currently serve tribal members. During his tenure in office, a written accounting of the capture of Jacob Knisely in 1778 was found in an Ohio History Book, written in 1884. In the chapter titled "The History of Wyandot County, Ohio", the accounting stated that Crow, or Jacob Knisely, was taken by the Wyandots at Loyal Hannah, Pennsylvania, in 1778. At Sandusky, Ohio, Crow was transferred to the Senecas. The United States Government made treaties in 1831 with the Senecas to cede their lands in Ohio moving them west to the Neosho country in Oklahoma. Crow and his family moved west with them in 1832. The accounting of this move was the first written history of the capture of Jacob Knisely known to the Whitecrow descendents and provided important family information for the Whitecrow genealogy.

In 1981, Leora (Lacie) Whitecrow, wife of Sid Whitecrow, was employed by the Department of the Interior, Bureau of Indian Affairs and began her research of the Whitecrow family from the myriad of records. After having worked on the genealogy of the Whitecrow family and realizing there were many people living who probably did not know they were related, Leora decided it was time for a gathering of the descendents of Tsu-ka-we or Crow. In 1999, planning began for the first ever Whitecrow Gathering in August of the year during the Green Corn ceremonies. Leora wanted to invite as many of the living descendents as could be located. Having the Knisely name from the written accounting, she searched the Internet for all the Knisely's in Pennsylvania. There was a Jacob Knisely listed with an address in Bellefonte, Pennsylvania. She wrote asking if he were interested in corresponding about family genealogy. He responded and they shared their family information. They learned that the family name has many different spellings and that there were large reunions and much research already completed on the Knisely families. Over the next year, phone calls and correspondence were shared with a strong bond of family being formed with Jake and Sondra Knisely.

Upon invitation, Jake and Sondra Knisely went to Oklahoma the following year to meet the Whitecrow family and attend their reunion and Green Corn ceremonies. Talk of family history only heightened the desire Leora Whitecrow had to do further research for the family of Jacob Knisely to learn who his parents and siblings were, where they lived and to learn if there were living descendents. Jake and Sondra promised to assist with the research in the Pennsylvania area. However Jake did not get the time to do the research as he had intended. In the summer of 2003, the Knisely's and Whitecrows were able to have a brief visit again in Miami, Oklahoma. They reminded Jake of his promise to look in PA and he and Sondra left from this short visit with a renewed determination to look for information in Greensburg, Pennsylvania.

The Nicely Family Search

In 1998, the author decided to begin gathering data on the Nicely family. A lot of data was already available from his mother Florence McDowell Nicely, who over many years had collected as much information as she could from family members about Jacob's oldest brother Anthony Kneisle and his branch of the family tree. This information was also taken from the memories of many of the living descendents of Anthony Nicely, just as with the Whitecrow family information. The search was expanded to include census records, church records, cemetery records, land records, and Internet genealogy sites. I spent a lot of time in the Westmoreland County Historical Society library going through the library of information available there. I also found a lot of information in the Westmoreland County Old and New History Books. Through family connections and the internet, I located Jack Nicely and Todd Pelkey, who had gathered a large amount of data on Jacob's brother Adam Kneisle Jr.'s side of the family tree. We now had information on Jacob's two brothers and their descendents and information on Jacob's capture, but we did not have any information on Jacob's descendents. The only information we had was from the history report from 1825 indicating that he had a family.

The old family story of the capture fascinated me, so in Calendar 2000, I decided to locate the farm and try to figure out how and where the capture took place. My Uncle Glenn Nicely contacted an individual, Duffy Johnson, who had lived in the Darlington area all of his life and had hunted through the farms in the area. Subsequently, we met with Johnson and he took us through the Four-Mile Run area showing us the location of the original Nicely farm and all sites of interest near the farm. He pointed out the fording site of the wagon road used to cross Four-Mile Run into the Fuller Nicely Hollow and the approximate location of the old wagon trail as it wound through the area. We did not stop at the farm on that first visit, just looked around briefly and left. Several weeks later, I went back to the farm and met the individual who was living there and farming the land. His name was George Bossart. I introduced myself and explained my interest in the farm. I told him the house that he was living in was built by my Three Great Grandfather Anthony Kneisle. I told him the purpose of my visit was to find anything and everything I could about the capture that took place somewhere on the farm. I was also interested in locating the site of the original log home. As soon as I mentioned the Indian capture he indicated that he knew the story and had also known that it had happened on the farm. He pointed to the lower field below the barn and indicated there was a blackberry patch at the lower end of the field and it was the only one he knew of on the farm. The patch was located just up the hill from Four-Mile Run.

For several years I had thought this berry patch was where the children were picking berries on the day of the capture. During 2001 and 2002, several other Nicely family members came to visit and I took them on a tour of the farm pointing out what was thought to be the capture site and the berry patch. However, after searching for more information on the location of the original log home in 2004 and locating it, again with information supplied by Duffy Johnson, our original assumptions about the capture location and the site of the berry patch could not have been correct. This berry patch is located over ¾ of a mile away from the original house location. It is also on the other side of a large hill. In addition the fields between the house and the indicated berry patch were not cleared until after 1775. The berry patch where the children were picking berries in 1775 would most likely have been within several hundred yards of the original log house.

There were trees all around the original home, which was built on a western slope of the land grant. This location was chosen because of the spring that was in close proximity, which would have supplied them with much needed water. Finding a good spring was a high priority for establishing a homesite. The home would have been well hidden in the area where it was located and probably gave them a feeling of security. From the home it was about one and ½ mile down the hill through the hollow to the Forbes Road and to Four-Mile Run. This was also where their wagon road was located and the most likely escape route for the Wyandot Indians when they captured Jacob. In fact the output from the spring continues down the hill gradually turning into a small stream as it picks up the output from other springs along the way. The stream then spills into the Four-Mile Run.

I now had everything I needed except a name to track down the descendents of Jacob. I began putting notes out on the Internet on several sites. I also went to the Westmoreland

County Historical Society, in 2000, and put some information in the research folder on the Nicely family, indicating that I had a lot more. Additionally I left information so that someone could get in touch with me. I thought the only way I might find them is if they found me! It was a long shot, but in the end that is exactly what happened.

The Mystery Unfolds

On August 28, 2003, Jake and Sondra Knisely made good on their promise by visiting the Westmoreland County Historical Society in Greensburg, PA to check through the records. When he entered the Westmoreland County Historical Society, he told the aides he was looking for information on the Knisely family, not spelling out his name but pronouncing it as Nicely, which is a prominent name in the Greensburg area. A local school in Greensburg was named Nicely Elementary in honor of Dr. Robert Francis Nicely Sr., who had been the Superintendent of the Greensburg Salem School District for a number of years. This was another of the small coincidences in this search that led to the aides at the Society pulling out the folder on the Nicely family. I am not sure if they would have found the file if he had spelled out his name instead of pronouncing it. Jake was not aware of the name being spelled as Nicely. As the aides were laying out a stack of Census books, Jake knew he and Sondra were not going to have time to go through all the material. However the aide also brought out the Nicely folder from their name file and in it they found a little blue post-em note attached to a letter. The note had a date of February 8, 2000 showing my name, address, telephone number, and Email address stating that I had information on 321 Nicely names and over 1,100 names of direct relatives of the Nicely family. The note also stated that the file was available in GEDCOM format.

As soon as Jake saw the note, he told them to stop looking as he was going to call me, before going any further. He called my home and my wife answered. He asked, "Is this the Nicely that has a lot of information on the Nicely family". My wife said, "Yes it was". He gave her his name and pointed out that it was spelled differently. He wanted to know specifically if I had any information on the capture of a Jacob Knisely by the Indians. She indicated that I did and that I had taken her past the site in recent weeks. My wife sensed a sound of excitement in his voice as he said, "You mean he even knows the place where the capture took place!" He indicated that he wanted to meet with me today if possible. She told him I would not be home until 4:00 PM giving him directions to our home.

At that point, my wife called me at the Compass Inn Museum in Laughlintown, where I was working as a volunteer docent telling me about Jake Knisely's call indicating to me the difference in the spelling of the name, and asking about the Indian capture. I also became excited because I connected the name with that of Jacob Kneisle and thought Jake might be a direct descendent of Jacob. Was this the connection I needed to complete the search for Jacob's family? Jake was so anxious to see me that he showed up at our home at 2:30 PM telling my wife that he and his wife would sit in the car until I got home. She invited them in spending an hour and a half with them before I got there. I walked in wearing the 1800 farmer's costume I wear at Compass Inn Museum and said, "I'm Ron Nicely and as you can see I am into history." Jake laughed and said, "I'm Jake Knisely, spelled Knisely and I am so pleased to meet you." I then said, "The next question is, are you related to the Jacob that was captured?" He replied "No, but I know the people who are." What an exciting moment that was. Chills still run up and down my spine every time I think about it.

We then began to talk about the descendents of Jacob, the Whitecrow family from Oklahoma, and he told me what he knew about them. I told him everything I knew about Jacob and the capture. We also talked about Jake's ancestors and tried to see if there were any connections to our family of Nicely's. We were not able at that time to make a connection but later on through DNA testing we established a link. This occurred after the original writing of the book. We now have a positive connection to the Knusli family tree. Jake then gave me the Whitecrow's address, phone number, and Email address. He then asked me to give him a couple of days before calling them because he wanted to be the one who told them their search was at an end. Jake and Sondra also wanted to return to the area when they had time in order to see the farm where the capture had taken place. We set up a date of September 10, 2003 for their visit and we subsequently traveled through the Four-Mile Run and the Ligonier area visiting the farm, the cemeteries and other areas around Ligonier. About a week later the connection between the Whitecrow family and myself was made and we began to exchange genealogy information on our respective families. The information sent to me included some history reports on Jacob's life as an Indian and a list of over two hundred of his descendents. As a result, we began to gain some insight into what had happened to Jacob after his father and friends had lost his trail near Saltsburg, Pennsylvania.

The information helped clear up some of the differences that I could not explain in the history accounts in the Westmoreland County History books. I had known that Jacob was born in 1770, but the historical report indicated he had been captured in 1790 at the age of 5. Until I saw this report from them showing the date of capture as 1778, I worked under the assumption that the original Jacob had died and the next son born was named Jacob, a common tradition in that time period. Since they had 1778 as the date of capture and that he was 5 years old, I used his birth information as a basis for the 1775 capture. Both reports had his age as 5 and the birth information showed that he was born in 1770. The information the Whitecrow family supplied on the 1825 meeting said it had been Jacob's father who came to visit him while the Westmoreland County History Book indicated it had been his brother. Since the records clearly show that his father Adam Sr. was age 95 in 1825 it would not have been likely that he could have made such a long journey on horseback. Since the Ohio newspaper report talked about his father being Adam, it was most likely Jacob's brother Adam Jr. who had rode to visit with him. The family tie was made and we had now connected the two branches of the family tree. The rest of the story could now be told for all to know!

CHAPTER FIVE

The Rest of the Story: Crow's Life

The Indians who captured Jacob and took him from the farm along Four-Mile Run were Wyandot Indians. The escape route was down Four-Mile Run then along the Loyalhanna Creek to the junction with the Kiskiminetas River. At the location of the current town of Saltsburg, there was an Indian

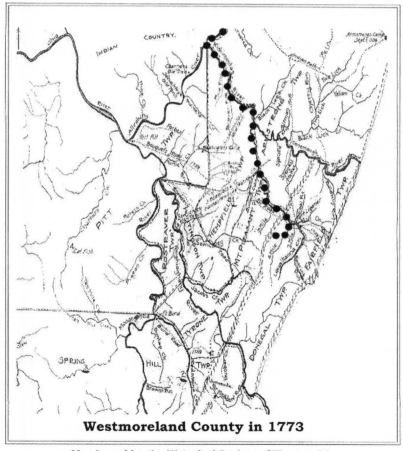

Westmoreland County in 1773

Map Issued by the Historical Society of Western PA

trail which was traveled by foot and traveled over a hill at what is now North Vandergrift and eventually comes out at Stitts Run which enters the Kiskiminetas River right across from what was Shawnee Old Town. It was probably their first stop after capturing Jacob and they may have stayed overnight at Shawnee Old Town, which is about a mile west of current city of Leechburg. They most likely proceeded the next day by canoe along the Kiskiminetas River to the point where it joined the Ohio River and then headed north in Pennsylvania along the Ohio River. Today that section of the Ohio River carries the name Allegheny River from the juncture at Pittsburgh to the north. The route is shown as dots on the map on the preceding page. At some point, beyond the coverage of this map, they took the Ohio River north to the French Creek at current day Venango then headed to the west and Lake Erie and ended their journey near the current location of Sandusky, Ohio. The entire trip was over 270 miles and it is difficult to estimate how long it took to make this journey. They probably made camp several times along the way for rest and made diversions to evade anyone seeing them and or following them. It is difficult for us to even imagine the fear and exhaustion Jacob suffered during this journey. A fear of the unknown is the worst fear we face in life and I'm sure little Jacob did not know what would happen to him. Additionally, the Indians probably could not explain to him what was going to happen due to the language barrier. It had to be a heart rending and fear filled trip for him. He had to be a terribly frightened little boy. He also was on a long walk and I'm sure his short legs had a hard time keeping up. Perhaps he was carried from time to time. It had to be very exhausting and his fear probably kept him from sleeping soundly. When they reached the main camp near Sandusky, Ohio, a Wyandot Indian woman, who became his adopted mother, would now raise him as her own child. Jacob's life as part of a loving pioneer family changed with his capture as a small boy. A choice he did not make. His legacy now became that of a Seneca Indian, who was a part of the Senecas of Sandusky.

Descendents of his family were told his name was Crow because "when he cried, he sounded like a crow". It is an assumption that the name of Crow is a conversion of the name Tsu-ka-we from the Wyandot language. The name Tsu-ka-we is not Seneca as far as is known. We also are unsure of when he was transferred to the Senecas. His adopted Wyandot mother began the process of training him in the ways of the Indians, schooling him in the language and the customs. Over time he grew to accept their customs and traditions. He was taught to farm, hunt and fish and many other skills necessary for his survival. Even Daniel Boone, who was captured, by the Shawnee Indian Tribe in 1778, and lived with the tribe for about six months, had adopted Indian customs during this period in his life. Boone escaped from the tribe in order to alert the settlers at Boonesborough that the Shawnee were planning a surprise attack on the fort. He later indicated he had been treated well and had felt very comfortable living with the Indians. Jacob soon became adapted to his new life as Tsu-ka-we living as a Seneca Indian in the area near Sandusky, Ohio.

Crow, as he grew older developed a skill as a great deer hunter. This was an important occupation in this time period, since the meat was used for food and the skins were used for clothing and for trading purposes. Davy Crockett and Daniel Boone were considered to be great hero hunters during this period of time, so it was a noble and prominent profession. Crow used a method for hunting deer after dark, shooting many fine bucks late at night. He would carry a pole seven feet long, pointed at the bottom end, and a fork at the upper end. Holding the pole with the fork towards the sky, he would mount a piece of bark, about fifteen inches wide and two feet long, to the fork so as to make the bottom level and the other end sticking up along the pole, like the letter L. A candle was placed on the level bottom piece of the bark. When the candle was lit and the stick held up over Crow's head, it cast a shadow on Crow as he held the stick and cast a light on objects in the distance. This would enable him to spot his game. The deer could see the light but they could not see Crow. When Crow located a deer, he would stick the pole in the soft ground, and making sure of his target, he would shoot the deer. This was called "fire hunting", and Crow would travel along the edges of the river, where the deer would come down to drink and find "salt licks".

Little Crow grew into manhood and took a Wyandot Indian as his first wife. We do not have any information on her name, but we do know she had two sons to Crow.

His first son, born in 1814, was named White Crow, probably due to the fact that his father was a white man or perhaps his skin was lighter in complexion. Later in life, White Crow would accumulate some wealth and adopted his father's name first name as Jacob and became known in records as Jacob Whitecrow and on occasion as Jacob Knisely. He became a successful trader with whites and with Indians, dressing as a white man and calling himself Jacob Knisely and dressing as an Indian and calling himself Jacob Whitecrow. Jacob Whitecrow, was married to Theresa Big Arms circa 1837. Theresa had been married to James Armstrong and had a son named James Armstrong Jr. circa 1834. She had seven children, two sons and five daughters to White Crow. All of the children used Whitecrow as their last name. Jacob was born on May 10 1838. Next born was a son, Leander born in 1840, then two daughters, Betsy born in 1844, and then Mary Jane born in 1846. Joseph (Indian name Ta-Ha-

Tse-Sa-Tes) his second son was born in 1848 along with a twin sister Lucinda (Lucy).

Crow's second son, born circa 1815, was named Jerry (Indian name Soh-Wah-Soh-Ses) Crow. Jerry was married twice. There is no record of his first wife's name. She had four children to Jerry. There were two daughters, an infant thought to be a daughter and a son. These children all carried the last name of Crow. The first daughter was Lucy born about 1836, followed by Mary born about 1838. Their third child was an unnamed infant, thought to be a daughter, born about 1840. The fourth child was a son named Joseph who was born about 1842. Jerry married a second wife Koh-Wah-Sa-Ni-Ah. They did not have any children.

Crow's second wife was the daughter (name unknown) of William Spicer, who was also a captured white boy and was also raised by the Indians. They did not have any children.

Crow's third wife was a Cayuga or Oneida woman. They had a son named Moses Crow, who was born circa 1817 and a daughter Cah-Quee-Nah, who was born circa 1818.

Moses Crow married Nancy (Indian name Ga-Na-Sa-Tah) last name unknown. They had five children, three sons and 2 daughters. These children used Crow as their last name. Their first son William was born about 1838. Their second child, a daughter, Mary (Indian name Ga-Na-Sa-Ta) was born circa 1840. Jane, their second daughter was born about 1852. Their fourth child, a son Amos was born about 1853. Their fifth child named John was born in 1857.

Crow's first daughter, Cah-Quee-Nah, to his third wife married Small Cloud Spicer, a son of William Spicer and a brother to Crow's second wife. She had four sons to Small Cloud. These boys used Spicer as their last name. George was born about 1833. Joseph was born in 1835. Daniel was born in 1840 and Armstrong was born in 1843.

Crow's fourth wife, whose name is not known, was from the Mohawk Indian Tribe. She had two daughters to Crow. The first daughter was born circa 1819 and her name was Wah-Deh-Dhyo-Do-Quah and a second daughter named Cah-Tee-Lih born circa 1821.

Wah-Deh-Dhyo-Do-Quah married John Winney and they had two sons and one daughter. These children carried the last name of their father Winney. James was born about 1840. Isaac was born in 1849 and Lizzie, a daughter was born about 1850.

Crow's second daughter Cah-Tee-Lih to his fourth wife was his last child. She married John Young and they had three daughters. These children carried Young as their last name. Snow was born about 1840, Ko-He-Ta-Gay was born about 1842, and Eliza (Indian name Kye-Whit-Ka-Ta) was born about 1844.

By 1825, Crow had three sons and three daughters and owned some land and other possessions and was living with the Senecas of Sandusky in Ohio. At this time in his life at age 55, he had probably given up any hope of finding his relatives from the Kneisle family in Pennsylvania. They were probably a fading memory and he no longer gave much thought to them. However this was all about to change. A trader, who was in the Sandusky area trading with the Senecas, noticed how much Crow resembled the Kneisle family. Being familiar with the story of the capture of Jacob, he struck up a conversation with Crow. During the conversation, the trader found out that Crow was indeed the captured boy Jacob Kneisle. The trader returned to the Ligonier Valley and reported to Jacob's father and mother what he had found. So his father Adam Sr. asked Adam Jr. to travel to Ohio and meet with Jacob and ask him to return to see his mother. He gathered provisions and set out on horseback to visit with Jacob.

The meeting with Jacob did not start off well. First, Jacob or Crow did not speak English and his brother did not speak Crow's language. They had to send for an interpreter to be able to talk. Jacob's brother related all of the information about the capture so he could confirm that he was really talking to Jacob. At first Crow denied every indication of his white heritage and of being the Jacob who was captured many years before. Finally his brother said, "If you are my brother then your name is Jacob." With this, Crow jumped up and said, "That is my name, and I am your brother; I recollect that, but I kept it all to myself for fear that somebody would claim me and take me away." Crow then sent to the Wyandot camp and had his adopted mother come to the meeting, who corroborated Mr. Kneisle's version of the capture of his brother. She was a very old squaw, and stayed several days, and as long as Mr. Kneisle stayed, to satisfy herself that Crow would not go back with his brother. Mr. Kneisle tried everything possible to induce his brother to go back with him to Pennsylvania. He told him that his mother had been sick for some time and was still mourning for her lost child for all of these years. Crow was immovable since he now had a family of his own to look after and could not go, but promised to visit his mother at a later time. He laughed heartily over the idea about how he would look dressed like a white man. Mr. Kneisle left one morning, and Crow accompanied his brother as far as Bellevue, Ohio, where they stayed together all night. They parted company the next morning and each returned to his own home. Crow never made the trip back to see his mother, who passed away in about 1829, never having seen her son again.

In 1831 as a result of a treaty, the lands owned by the Senecas of Ohio were ceded to the United States Government. The sale of Crow's property and improvements, as a result of the treaty, brought him a sum of $950.00. In addition, another

Indian paid off a debt he owed to Crow in the amount of $50.00. This left Crow very well off for a man in that period of time. In 1832, the U. S. Government moved the Senecas of Ohio to a reservation in what is now Oklahoma. This was a journey of approximately 1,000 miles. Crow made the decision to make the trip to the new reservation. He was not forced into making this choice. It may have been the apparent restless pioneer spirit of the Kneisle family surging in his mind and body that made him chose to make this journey. The trip west was made by covered wagons. Travel by wagon train was a slow and hazardous process. Many members of the traveling party died due to illness and accidents during the trip to the new reservation. The horses had to be rested, fed, and watered during the trip. The members of the wagon train had to hunt for and prepare their food at the end of each day. Roads were in poor condition and there were rivers to cross and mud holes in which to get stuck and mountains to climb. On a good day they might make ten miles, on some days fewer. They were at the mercy of the weather as they made this long journey. This was a trip that may have taken four months or longer to reach their destination.

Sadly Crow became afflicted with Cholera shortly after arriving in Oklahoma dying at the age of 63 in 1833. It was the second time in his life that he was taken from his family and once again his surviving descendents mourned him.

The meeting with Jacob in 1825 was the first of two historic meeting for this family. The next meeting would occur on October 4, 2003, 228 years and approximately 2 months after the original capture in 1775. What reaction would the families experience at the meeting in 2003?

CHAPTER SIX

The Reunion

Several days after exchanging genealogy information with the Whitecrow family, it was determined that Sidney, Jay and Virginia were my 5th cousins, having in common our Four Great Grandparents, Adam and Elizabeth Eichert Kneisle (Nicely) Sr., who had three sons named Anthony, Adam Jr., and Jacob. The Ligonier area Nicely descendents were members of either Anthony or Adam Jr.'s family, whereas the Whitecrow and Crow families were descendents of Jacob. Adam Sr. and Elizabeth also had five daughters, but at the current time I have only two of these branches partially developed. Since Virginia Wood, who had started this search over 20 years ago was having some health problems, the family decided to make a trip to the Ligonier area as soon as possible, so that they could bring her with them. They were afraid that time might make it more difficult for her to visit. We set a date of October 3, 2003 and agreed that I would take them on a tour of the Ligonier area showing them the capture site, the cemeteries and arrange for them to meet some of the Ligonier relatives.

They arrived on Friday evening with our first meeting being at the Eat n Park restaurant near Latrobe. After dinner, they followed me to my home to visit for an hour making arrangements to do the tour in the morning. In the meantime, another 5th cousin, who I had met through the Internet, had decided to come from Las Vegas to visit at the same time. Bill Frederick was a descendent of the Adam Nicely Jr. family branch and was a 5th cousin to both the Whitecrow family and to myself. I had taken him on a tour earlier in the day on Friday, but he decided he would like to go on the tour with the Whitecrow family on Saturday also. Jake Knisely and his wife Sondra also joined the tour.

On Oct 4th, we started our tour from the Wingate Inn, near Latrobe, traveling on Route 30 towards Ligonier. Along the way to Ligonier we were able to see the Loyalhanna Creek to our left. It was along this creek that Jacob was taken by the Wyandot Indians when they captured him. We turned off Route 30 before Longbridge, the bridge on Route 30 that crosses over the Loyalhanna Creek. We traveled through the village of Darlington arriving at the Keltz Cemetery on the other side of Darlington. The headstone of Jacob's father is located just inside the gate and to the left. There is no indication of Jacob's mother Elizabeth on the headstone with Adam Sr. and no record on the cemetery listing, but we feel sure she would have been buried in the same plot with Adam Sr. We also saw the headstone of Jacob's brother Anthony and again his wife Sarah is not listed on the headstone or in the cemetery records, but we feel quite sure she is buried in the same plot as Anthony. We also saw the headstone of George Keltz who was Jacob's Godfather. Jacob's Godmother was Anna Maria Eager Keltz, the wife of George Keltz. Again there is no indication on the headstone of Anna Maria being buried in the same plot, but we feel sure she is also buried along with George. We then proceeded to the site of the original Nicely homestead, which is where the capture took place. It is located near Four-Mile Run, in back of Darlington on the Chestnut Ridge. We were able to see the house that Jacob's brother Anthony built in 1810. There is still a barn there but it is a reconstructed barn built on the foundation that Anthony built. A fire had destroyed the 1810 barn that Anthony had built. While at the farm a photographer from the Latrobe Bulletin joined us to take photos of the event for publication in the newspaper. The group then traveled to the site of Jacob's brother Adam Jr.'s house and barn near Route

711 south of Ligonier. Later we visited the Ligonier Valley cemetery where many members of the Nicely family are buried. We traveled to the home of my Uncle Glenn Nicely located on Nicely Road, the home where I was born. We visited with Glenn and my Aunt Anna Ruth Nicely Demmitt. We then visited my Aunt Mary Nicely Armor who lived in Ligonier on Main Street. After a visit there we went to the Diamond in Ligonier and they looked through the shops for souvenirs of the Ligonier area.

At 6:00 PM that evening, we all came together for a mini family reunion at The Driftwood near Ligonier. We had arranged for 39 of our relatives to meet there for a buffet dinner and a chance to get to know the Whitecrow family. We had 35 local Valley relatives, 3 relatives from Philadelphia, Jack Nicely's family, plus Bill Frederick from Las Vegas, Jake and Sondra Knisely, and the 6 members of the Whitecrow family. It was indeed a magical and emotional evening. The Whitecrow's felt like and were accepted as members of our family from the first moment we met. There was a special feeling of kinship between all of the relatives present at that reunion. Everyone indicated that they felt like they had known the Whitecrow family members all of their lives. The atmosphere at the reunion was magical to say the least. I made a presentation covering the basic information about how we had met and connected and thanked my Mother Florence McDowell Nicely and Virginia Scritchfield (Whitecrow) Wood for taking the time to gather all of this family information. I also thanked Jake and Sondra Knisely for helping to get us together. I then introduced each of the Whitecrow family members and had everyone come past and meet them. An unexpected event then happened that took me totally by surprise. They honored me in a small ceremony by presenting me with an Indian blanket of friendship. There was a ceremonial presentation of draping the blanket over my shoulders by Shawna Whitecrow Adams, dressed in her native Indian dress. This was followed by a Lulu. This left me choked up and my wife and sister crying tears of joy over the honor bestowed on me. There was a reporter from the Ligonier Echo in attendance and she took pictures and recorded the event for publication in the newspaper.

The Lulu is a sound made by the women to show appreciation, approval or support. When someone dances from the heart, a song touches you, for instance or as a sign of appreciation (the Friendship Blanket and the ties to the new found "old" family) is when this sound is appropriate. It is often done as a sign of thanks for a gift you've received during a "giveaway" ceremony at a pow-wow. The sound is made is by saying the word, Lu lu lu lu in succession, usually very rapidly with the front edge of the tongue using a comfortable (usually high) pitch. The length of time the sound is made is based on the air capacity of the person and the particular situation. Men don't Lulu – it's strictly a woman's sound. Men use a war hoop, which has a slightly different sound and is used as a means of intimidating your enemy.

Leora Whitecrow then read a poem she wrote about Jacob titled "A Man of Two Lives". It left most us with tears in our eyes. Jay Whitecrow then honored me with a Walking Staff with an eagle head carved at the top of the handle. A buffet was available and after the meal there was a lot of picture taking with all members of the extended families involved. Everyone there had a great time and the family bonding was unbelievable. This was the culmination of a 20 plus year search by the Whitecrow family as they looked for the site of the capture of Crow, to see where he was born. For us it was the culmination of our search and questions of what had happened to Jacob Kneisle, captured 228 years earlier. The story has now reached a satisfying conclusion. The family relationships we have established will live on in the future with visits to Oklahoma and future visits to the Ligonier Valley. A group went to Oklahoma in 2004 and attended the Whitecrow family reunion and their Greencorn Ceremony. Sid and Leora were in Ligonier in 2007 to attend a gravestone dedication ceremony by the Sons of the American Revolution for Adam Nicely at the Keltz Cemetery. We had a small gathering the evening before the ceremony at our home near Latrobe. We also made a visit to the original homesite, after the ceremony, which was discovered after the Whitecrows were here in 2004. Between the homesite and Adam Sr.'s original springhouse, a black crow feather was found in the area in front of Leora Whitecrow's path through the woods. The tip was pointing at her indicating the feather was meant for her. When she picked it up, she closed her eyes and later said little Jakey told her this was the site of the capture. It was a thrilling and exciting event for the 15 members of the family who made this trip with us.

Sid and Leora returned in 2009 and brought five other Whitecrow family members with them to see the area where the events of the capture took place. We spent the day together and had a small gathering at our home near Latrobe, before they left.

CHAPTER SEVEN

Other Indian Captures

The capture of Jacob Kneisle was not the only capture in and around the Ligonier Valley. There were many other reported instances of captures. Some of these were also included in the Westmoreland County History Books. The stories that follow were reported in Volume 1, Chapter 7, in Part 1 and 2. There are many other family stories of captures and conflicts in the area around Ligonier during this period of time, some were recorded and some were told and retold and passed down from generations to generation within the family. You can read more of these stories by accessing the pa-roots.com web site on the Internet. Select Pennsylvania and click on the Westmoreland County section. If you click on the History Project link, the available chapters can be found. Not all the chapters have been retyped and transferred to the web site, but it is a work in progress. Eventually they want to have all the chapters converted and available for viewing. Several of these recorded stories are included below. Please keep in mind that all but the last story included here took place during the Revolutionary War.

The Harman Family

The Harman family was another family that suffered greatly from the Indians. They lived near the William's Blockhouse along Four-Mile Run, several miles further upstream than the Kneisle homestead. Their story is also heart rending. Their family had also moved to the area early and was known to be living there in 1776. They probably were there much earlier, just as the Kneisle family had moved in to the area around 1761. Their story began in 1777 as Harman and two of his friends were riding to their home on horseback. Several Indians were hiding along the trail and shot and killed all three of the men.

Harman's widow was left with his land along Four-Mile Run, which included the mouth of Laurel Run and three sons, Andrew, John, and Phillip, with Andrew the oldest at 14 years of age. They moved into the William's blockhouse for the winter and in the spring they moved back to the land to begin working the farm. One morning the widow saw some horses in their grain field and sent Andrew and John to drive off the horses. Three Indians were hiding nearby and easily captured John, but Andrew ran towards the house. He was quickly overtaken by one of the Indians, who threatened him with a raised tomahawk. He was taken back to join his brother and they were taken from the area. The Indians asked if there were men in the house and Andrew lied to them and told them there was. This probably saved the lives of his mother and youngest brother. They could hear their mother calling for them but were warned by the Indians if they cried out that they would be killed. They were made to travel with the Indians to Northern Pennsylvania. During the trip the Indians showed them a pocket watch, which was their father's watch taken from him when he was killed. It turned out that one of the Indians was in the group that had murdered their father during the previous year.

Once they reached the Seneca Village, they were adopted as members of the tribe and in general were treated well. During the year following their capture there was a lot of illness among the Indians and many died including Andrew's brother John Harman. The following year also brought much hardship to the Indian tribe and it was decided that Andrew should be killed so they would not have to feed him. They made several attempts to kill him but failed each time, so they decided not to kill him.

Two years after his capture, he was sold to a British officer for a bottle of rum and was taken back to London for two years to work as a servant for the officer. At the end of the Revolutionary War he was exchanged and was sent back to New York, from where he found his way back to the homestead on Four-Mile Run. His mother had remained on the farm and his youngest brother had grown and was taking care of the farm. When he walked into the home without warning his mother recognized him, was overcome with joy and fainted in his arms. The news of his return brought large crowds to his home. Many came because they did not believe the story and had to see for themselves. He and his mother lived together on the old homestead for many years. During the rest of his life he was a woodsman and enjoyed hunting. He walked with the gait of an Indian and was happy when traveling through the wilderness. He always spoke kindly of the Indians in spite of the evil suffered by his family.

The Campbell Family

Another incident that occurred near Pleasant Grove church, a short distance east of Mansville and the Four-Mile Run involved the family of Robert Campbell. Their home was about four miles southeast of the Nicely homestead. In July 1776, Robert and his brothers William and Thomas were working in their fields. There had not been any Indian raids for some time and so they were not guarded. As they worked a party of Indians appeared. The boys ran swiftly towards their home but were quickly overtaken. They were held captive while some of the Indians approached their home. Their mother, their 3 sisters and an infant child were still in the home. The mother saw them approaching and took the infant child and ran. The Indians overtook her and struck her down. When she fell the infant was crushed underneath her.

The Indians then gathered up the three sisters, Polly, Isabel, and Sarah. The Indians took the Campbell's horses and began the trip out of the valley with the boys walking and the girls riding on the back of the horses. However the youngest girl could not hold on and kept falling off the horse, so they killed her and moved on. The trip took a similar route to the one used in the capture of Jacob by heading north to Saltsburg and across the Kiskiminetas River and then north through Pennsylvania. However, this group was taken to New York.

Once in camp the children were separated. Thomas was sold to a British officer and taken to London. There is no indication that he returned to the valley. The two girls were held for four years and then returned to the valley. William returned to his home at the end of the Revolutionary War. Robert remained in captivity for six years before managing to escape and returned to his home in 1782. He lived out the rest of his life in the area and became well know as the leader of the Presbyterian Church at Pleasant Grove. He was known as the "Elder" Robert Campbell to separate him from others of the same name. His grave is in the Pleasant Grove Cemetery.

The Ulery Family

The Ulery family also lived in the general area of the Four-Mile Run. They were located 2 miles south of Fort Ligonier about a mile west of the road from Ligonier to Stahlstown along Slater Road and about 2 miles from the Nicely homestead. During the Revolutionary War they farmed their land and in times of danger they stayed at Fort Preservation in Ligonier. On a warm day in July, they were living at their home, since there had been no recent Indian attacks into the area. Three of the daughters were out raking some new mown hay. Abigail, Elizabeth, and Juliann Ulery were so busy with their work, they did not see a group of Indians sneaking up on them until they were very close to them. The girls took off running at once for their home. Juliann, 20 years of age and Elizabeth at 18 years of age outran Abigail, age 16, but she was very close behind. The two sisters thought Abigail had been captured and took the sound of her footsteps to be those of an Indian pursuer, causing them to run even faster. The two older girls upon reaching the house closed and barred the door. When Abigail reached the door she was not allowed to enter, since they thought she was one of the Indians. Due to her frightened condition, instead of yelling out, she ran around the house to the higher ground behind the house.

The Indians decided not to chase her and tried to break down the door. Their father grabbed his gun and fired through the door, wounding an Indian in the bowels. Since the door would not give way and fearing another shot through the door, they left the house and went in the direction that Abigail had ran. Abigail found a hiding place in a hole in the ground, where a large tree had been blown over during a storm. Leaves that had blown in and weeds that had grown there over time filled the hole and she concealed herself in the hole. She was only concealed for a few minutes until the Indians came upon the tree and began to search for her. The Indians however chose to search among the branches instead of at the root of the tree. She heard one of the Indians yell to the others to look closely because he could smell her and that they would kill her when they found her. She told others later that the most difficult thing she had ever done in her life was to stay still, because her first instinct was to jump up and run. Had she jumped and ran she would surely have been killed.

As it turned out the injured Indian helped to save Abigail. His moaning from the gunshot caused the others to cut their search short and they began to carry him away. As soon as she was sure they were gone, she ran rapidly to the cabin and was taken into the house. The family was surprised to see her fearing she was taken captive or killed.

But this was not to be the end of the story. Once the Indians had attacked an area, they normally did not return to that area giving it a clear berth for a period of time, so they assumed it would be safe to go to the fields again. As a result, Juliann and Elizabeth went back out to the same field to continue their work. Abigail was still too frightened to go with them. The Indians returned and circled around to cut off the escape path to the house and easily captured them. The Indians took them from their farm southeast in the direction of the current location of Brant's School. They dragged the girls most of the way since they were crying and overcome with grief. The Indians tried to calm them down by telling them they would be treated kindly if they went with them. When that did not work they threatened to kill them if they did not quiet down and go with them. The Indians were afraid the noise would bring a rescue group to help the girls. The girls were complaining that the briars and thorns were hurting their feet, so the Indians gave them moccasins to wear. Even then the girls impeded their escape so the Indians again gave them a choice of life or death which probably worsened their chances of quieting down. The Indians struck them with their tomahawks and scalped them, leaving them for dead.

The Indians left but soon returned since they had forgotten to take the moccasins they had given to the girls. Miraculously neither of the girls was dead as a result of being struck on the head and from the scalping. Unfortunately Elizabeth had recovered enough to sit up, but was too dazed to move. As a result she was struck again and killed. Juliann was still lying where they had left her but was unable to move, so they assumed she was dead and left the area. Her father found her the next day and she was taken home and cared for. She never completely recovered from her head wound and she was sickly most of the rest of her life. She lived with her sister Abigail for the rest of her life. Abigail married Isaac Slater and lived on her father's farm the rest of her life. She lived a full life and died at 89 years of age in 1855. She retold the story of her escape many times during her life. Two of Abigail's granddaughters were married to descendents of Adam Nicely Sr.

The following story is the only one included that was outside of the Revolutionary War time period. It began before Pontiac's War and ended at the battle of Fallen Timber. As in all groups of people there are those who act without respect for good morals and those who act out of compassion and kindness. The following story illustrates some of the compassion that occurs even in wartime. One Indian chose to show compassion and kindness to a pioneer family during a period of great strife during Pontiac's War and the attack on Fort Ligonier. A member of that pioneer family returned his good deed to him many years later after the battle at Fallen Timber.

Maidenfoot and Mary Means

The commander of Fort Ligonier in 1763 had several groups of Indians approach the fort claiming to be friendly and the commander and his men treated them with respect and kindness. On one of these visit, a young brave named Maidenfoot was with the group. During this particular visit to the fort, he saw the 11-year-old daughter of a pioneer named Means, whose family was staying at the fort for protection over the winter months. He was greatly taken by her and struck up a conversation with her. He found out that her family lived about a mile south of the fort, just off of the current Ligonier to Stahlstown road. Upon leaving the fort he gave a string of beads to the young girl, which was probably of great value to him. It was said he seemed sad and heartbroken as he talked to the girl. The girl kept the beads and wore them from time to time, because she found them attractive.

During late May or early June of the same year, Mrs. Means and her daughter had packed up their goods and were on the way to the fort, since there were warnings of Indian attacks in the area. Mr. Means had chosen to stay and protect his property. The girl was wearing her beads around her neck. Before they could reach the fort, they were captured by the Indians and taken into the woods and tied to a tree. They were told to be quiet or they would be killed. Shortly thereafter they could hear the sounds of a battle at the fort. It was Chief Pontiac's attack on Fort Ligonier. Later in the afternoon an Indian approached Mrs. Means and her daughter, perhaps to kill them and take their scalps. The Indian turned out to be Maidenfoot, who immediately recognized the girl and the beads he had given her. He immediately freed them and took them in the direction of their home. Mr. Means was still at the home and Maidenfoot told them to head for the mountains further to the south and they would be safe there. He went with them to ensure their safety. He told them to hide there for a short time after which the Indians would be gone and they could come back to their home. As he was leaving, he took the girl's handkerchief, which was white, and had her name "Mary Means" stitched in black silk.

Many years' later Mary's family moved to Ohio and she married an Army Officer named Kearney. Kearney commanded a company under General Anthony Wayne against the Indians at the battle at Fallen Timber. After the battle had ended, some of Kearney's men saw an elderly

Indian sitting on a log and waving a white cloth over his head. Some of Kearney's men wanted to shoot him but the captain stopped them. When he approached the Indian, the Indian told him them he had fought at Ligonier, at Bushy Run, at Hannastown, and at Wabash against St. Clair, and at Fallen Timber. He said he was old and tired and did not wish to fight anymore. He had done his share of fighting to defend his race, but now he wanted to live in peace with mankind. A search of his possessions revealed a handkerchief with the name of Kearney's wife Mary Means stitched in black silk. Having heard the story many times from his wife, Captain Kearney asked him for his name and found out it was Maidenfoot. He at once took Maidenfoot to his home to see his wife. Even though thirty-one years had passed they recognized each other immediately. All these years Mary had treasured her beads, because they had saved her life and Maidenfoot also treasured her handkerchief, but for a different reason. He was taken with Mary the first time he saw her because he had lost a younger sister about Mary's age and size just before he had met Mary at Fort Ligonier. He stayed with the Kearney family and settled in Ohio near the Kearney's and adapted to their customs. He died about 4 years later from consumption and was buried with military honors in a small church cemetery near Cincinnati, Ohio. His grave marker carries the following inscription. "In Memory of Maidenfoot, an Indian chief of the Eighteenth Century, who died a civilian and a Christian."

Conclusion

There were many incredible incidents involving the Kneisle family starting with their journey across the ocean. The family members were truly pioneers of early America. Their experience in the Ligonier Valley area during the period of time from 1761 till 1794 was one, which would have weakened most families and driven them out of the area. The constant pressure of not knowing what hazards and difficulties tomorrow would bring surely had to wear on them mentally.

The capture of their young son had to be extremely difficult for Adam Sr. and Elizabeth to bear the rest of their lives, but they managed to move on with their lives and work continuing to function for their family. Jacob or Crow as he became known proceeded with his life had a large family and prospered in his new environment. He was another example of the strength of spirit in this family. It also shows the kindness that was offered to Jacob by the Wyandot Indians in raising him into a well-respected individual.

The strength of all the pioneers discussed in this book shines through at every turn. The move of all these pioneers to American in the early 1700's and then venturing into wilderness in the late 1700's certainly shows this was not a venture for the weak. Life was difficult enough just establishing a homestead in the Frontier, without the constant threat of attacks and wars. All of us whose ancestors made this journey have much to be grateful for their efforts. Most of us would have failed under lesser trials and tribulations. Researching and writing this story was an enlightening experience. I found much more than I expected to find. I hope you find that reading this story has given you an understanding of the early settlers who helped establish this great country and on the history around the Four-Mile Run section of the Ligonier Valley.

APPENDIX A

Poems about Jacob and Crow

During the years the story of Jacob Kneisle generated a ballad and a poem. Virginia McAdoo Daniels, who was a former resident of Ligonier valley and a schoolteacher in the Latrobe School system, wrote the following Ballad. As I mentioned before the history of this event included some errors with regard to names and dates. She named the Ballad "The Ballad of Jake Nicely" which was more about the father and in the ballad called his son little Jake. Adam Nicely Sr. was Jacob's father as we found out many years later, so the title should have read "The Ballad of Adam Nicely". The ballad is rather haunting and shows the sadness that was part of the memory of the capture. The Ballad was originally published in the Ligonier Echo.

THE BALLAD OF JAKE NICELY

(A tale of Ligonier Valley) written in 1948
By Virginia McAdoo Daniels
(Former resident of Ligonier Valley)

There lived a man on Four Mile Run,
He was a pioneer;
The Indians stole his little son,
His five year old son, so dear.

Away through the forest path they ride,
Through jungles of fern and dew,
Through tangled vines and rivers wide'
No slumber their eyelids knew.

64

But little Jake in Indian camp,
Lived in the sun and dew,
Where all night long on his blanket damp,
He forgot each name he knew.

The new moons came, would wax and wane,
He married as most men do,
An Indian squaw not far from Kane,
And they were happy, too.

The father frail still searched the trail;
The years were now two score,
He met this man so strong and hale,
But his son returned no more.

And often by the fire-fly's light,
When you hear the whip-poor-will,
On Four-Mile Run, they say, each night,
You can see him searching still.

Shortly after Virginia Daniels' ballad was published Effie Ryan Everett wrote a reply to the ballad with her own poem. Again the information on the father's name was incorrect in the history, since she also used Jake as the name of the father.

SAY THE GHOST OF JAKE NICELY

(Written by the late Effie Ryan Everett, in 1948,
in reply to "The Ballad of Jake Nicely"
by Virginia McAdoo Daniels)

How weary the ghost of Jake Nicely must be,
As lonely he wanders, never free

To lay him down in deep quiet sleep,
But ever his watchful vigil keep.

Folks say – those who live near the Four-Mile Run –
That he searches still for his little son,
Who was carried away so long ago
By Indians, then the white man's foe.

Perhaps some night when the stars hang low,
And the moon sheds a mystic, magic glow,
Somehow he may end his weary quest,
And find at last deep, dreamless rest.

When we had our Whitecrow – Nicely reunion in Ligonier on October 3rd, Leora Lacie Whitecrow, the wife of Sidney Whitecrow, read a poem that she had written after reading the stories about Jacob's capture and the ballad and the poem. She also knew the history of the man Tsu-ka-we or Crow that the boy Jacob Kneisle grew up to be. The poem brought tears to the eyes of many during the reading. The poem is about a man of two lives.

<u>A MAN OF TWO LIVES</u>

It now seems so very long ago,
But in Westmoreland County, it never grew old,
Questions still were asked and speculation made,
Of what happened to little Jakey Kneisle, Oh, how sad.

Scared and helpless on the Four Mile Run
A child was taken, it was Adam and Elizabeth's son,
To understand the reasons would be incomprehensible,
That one could replace another was not even sensible.

Jakey was accepted and raised by someone who,
Had lost someone also, a tradition they knew.
She called him Tsu-Ka-We, or Crow, his English name,
She taught him the language and he became the same.

With the Senecas in Sandusky he grew into a man,
Had a family and prospered from working the land.
His children were educated and added their part,
To a changing world that westward would start.

In 1832, Tsu-Ka-We moved to the country of Neosha,
Among other Senecas and Cayugas he would go.
In 1833, he was sick with cholera, from which he died,
Again he was mourned and his family cried.

His sons were White Crow, Moses Crow, and Jerry,
His daughters were three and had families who married,
Grandchildren were born and the lineage has grown,
To at least nine generations and still going strong.

Throughout it all, little Jakey was guided by Ya-Weh,
Who, we believe, had a hand in us gathering today,
Joining his two families at this historic time and place,
Giving us a chance to love each other and come face to face.

E-scong-e-ite (I will see you again)

APPENDIX B

Descendants of Adam and Elizabeth Eichert Kneisle (Nicely) Sr. for Four Generations

1-Adam NICELY (NUSLI) Sr. (1730-1826)
+Elizabeth EICHERT (1735-abt 1830)
. . . . .2-Anthony NICELY (NUSLI) Sr. (abt 1758-4 Dec 1845)
. . . . . +Sarah Salome HARGNETT (abt 1775-abt 1849)
. . . . 3-Anthony Wayne NICELY (NUSLI)
. . . . (2 Aug 1806-3 Jun 1891)
. . . . +Rosanna Maria KELTZ (22 Feb 1811-3 Jan 1886)
. . . . .4-Sarah NICELY (NUSLI)
. . . . (30 May 1831-bef 1921)
. . . . .4-Adam NICELY (NUSLI)
. . . . (4 Apr 1833-3 Mar 1873)
. . . . .4-John Hargnett (Drover) NICELY (NUSLI)
. . . . (30 Aug 1835-8 Oct 1916)
. . . . .4-Barbara NICELY (NUSLI) (1837-bef 1927)
. . . . .4-Lovina Jane NICELY (NUSLI)
. . . . (6 Apr 1838-Oct 1919)
. . . . .4-William H. NICELY (NUSLI)
. . . . (1841- 30 Aug 1862)
. . . . .4-Mary E. NICELY (NUSLI) (1843-bef 1933)
. . . . .4-Eliza NICELY (NUSLI) (1846-bef 1860)
. . . . .4-Harriet NICELY (NUSLI) (1848-bef 1938)
. . . . .4-Joseph NICELY (NUSLI) (1851-bef 1931)
. . . . 3-George NICELY (NUSLI) (Twin Eliza May)
. . . . (21 Mar 1810-14 Jun 1867)
. . . . +Sarah Ann BEST (14 Dec 1820-3 Nov 1901)
. . . . .4-Sarah Ann (Sadie) NICELY (NUSLI)
. . . . (Aug 1839-1 Nov 1901)
. . . . .4-Rebecca Jane NICELY (NUSLI)
. . . . (1841-16 Apr 1924)

. . . . .4-Anthony Wayne NICELY (NUSLI)
        (21 Mar 1842-18 Feb 1918)
. . . . .4-Jacob C. NICELY (NUSLI)
        (5 Dec 1844-21 Nov 1866)
. . . . .4-Rosanna Young NICELY (NUSLI)
        (5 May 1846-23 Nov 1872)
. . . . .4-Joseph B. NICELY (NUSLI)
        (4 Jun 1849-23 Mar 1852)
. . . . .4-Amanda Melisa NICELY (NUSLI)
        (30 Dec 1852-24 Apr 1941)
. . . . .4-Joseph NICELY (NUSLI) (1853-1919)
. . . . .4-George Allen Brown NICELY (NUSLI)
        (31 Jul 1857-5 Sep 1936)
. . . . .4-Kesiah NICELY (NUSLI) (1859-bef 1949)
. . . . 3-Eliza May (Mary) NICELY (NUSLI)
        (Twin George) (21 Mar 1810-13 Mar 1893)
. . . . +John AUKERMAN (ACKERMAN?)
        (abt 1809-bef 1889)
. . . . .4-Martha AUKERMAN (ACKERMAN?)
        (16 May 1846-bef 1936)
. . . . 3-Elizabeth NICELY (NUSLI)
        (5 Mar 1811-bef 1894)
. . . . +Henry or Sylvester MILLER (abt 1813-bef 1893)
. . . . .4-Elmina MILLER (14 Jun 1829-13 Nov 1916)
. . . . .4-Elizabeth MILLER (2 Mar 1831-Aug 1831)
. . . . .4-Ann Matida MILLER
        (14 Oct 1832-14 Jun 1848)
. . . . .4-Elivira Elizabeth MILLER
        (11 Oct 1834-30 Aug 1861)
. . . . .4-Westley Sylvester MILLER
        (30 Sep 1836-23 May 1910)
. . . . .4-Lucinda MILLER
        (11 Nov 1838-19 Dec 1865)
. . . . .4-Henry Harnet MILLER

(30 Sep 1840-15 Mar 1904)

. . . . 3-Adam NICELY (NUSLI)

(25 Nov 1812-6 Sep 1868)

. . . . +Rachel Ann BEST (18 Aug 1814-13 Dec 1873)

. . . . .4-Fuller John NICELY (NUSLI)

(2 Nov 1837-4 Feb 1913)

. . . . .4-Margaret NICELY (NUSLI)

(5 Jul 1838-Feb 1891)

. . . . .4-Asher K. NICELY (NUSLI)

(Apr 1839-6 Mar 1898)

. . . . .4-Sarah NICELY (NUSLI)

(Jun 1840-28 Sep 1900)

. . . . .4-Ann Elizabeth (Mary) NICELY (NUSLI)

(May 1843-11 Jun 1901)

. . . . .4-Anthony Snow NICELY (NUSLI)

(6 Oct 1844-11 Mar 1907)

. . . . .4-Mariah Best (Mariam) NICELY (NUSLI)

(1847-bef 1942)

. . . . .4-Samuel NICELY (NUSLI) (1849-bef 1939)

. . . . .4-Sarah K. N. A. NICELY (NUSLI)

(16 Nov 1851-10 May 1861)

. . . . .2-Rosanna NICELY (NUSLI) (abt 1763-bef 1844)

. . . . . +William E. KARNS (KERNS) (abt 1763-1838)

. . . . 3-Adam KARNS (KERN) (abt 1810-bef 1890)

. . . . +Catherine UNKNOWN (1814-bef 1894)

. . . . .2-Adam NICELY (NUSLI) Jr. (abt 1764-1838)

. . . . . +Mary Sarah? UNKNOWN (22 Feb 1778-1 Aug 1819)

. . . . 3-Margaret NICELY (NUSLI) (1800-1884)

. . . . +David Shannon ROBERTS

(3 Feb 1800-17 Jan 1856)

. . . . .4-John ROBERTS (abt 1823-abt 1846)

. . . . .4-Lewis ROBERTS

(21 Feb 1824-23 Mar 1915)

. . . . .4-Adam ROBERTS (1827-bef 1917)

. . . . .4-Lavina ROBERTS (Mar 1830-22 Apr 1913)
. . . . .4-Jacob ROBERTS
          (20 Nov 1832-13 Nov 1908)
. . . . .4-Martha ROBERTS (1835-bef 1925)
. . . . .4-Robert R. ROBERTS (1837-bef 1927)
. . . . .4-Margaret ROBERTS
          (Apr 1840-16 Jan 1907)
. . . . .4-Matthew Shannon ROBERTS
          (8 Aug 1843-10 Oct 1865)
. . . . .4-Mary ROBERTS (2 Dec 1825-1 Feb 1899)
. . . . 3-Adam NICELY (NUSLI) (abt 1801-bef 1891)
. . . . 3-Elizabeth NICELY (NUSLI) (abt 1802-bef 1882)
. . . . +Peter MILLER (abt 1801-bef 1881)
. . . . 3-John Fuller (Sawdust) NICELY (NUSLI)
          (3 May 1803-24 Jun 1845)
. . . . +Sarah KNOX (1812-abt 1860)
. . . . .4-Maria Sarah NICELY (NUSLI)
          (1 Jun 1831-7 Jun 1863)
. . . . .4-Alexander NICELY (NUSLI)
          (1837-bef 1917)
. . . . .4-Rebecca N. NICELY (NUSLI)
          (10 Nov 1838-1915)
. . . . .4-George W. NICELY (NUSLI)
          (1842-bef 1922)
. . . . .4-Eliza J. NICELY (NUSLI) (1843-bef 1933)
. . . . .4-Margaret NICELY (NUSLI) (1844-bef 1934)
. . . . 3-Rosanna NICELY (NUSLI) (abt 1804-1892)
. . . . +Alexander MCDOWELL (abt 1802-bef 1886)
. . . . 3-George A. NICELY (NUSLI) Sr.
          (11 May 1805-14 Aug 1883)
. . . . +Eve GEORGE (14 Apr 1810-19 Dec 1890)
. . . . .4-John NICELY (NUSLI)
          (2 Nov 1837-4 Feb 1913)
. . . . .4-Sarah NICELY (NUSLI) (1840-bef 1930)

. . . . .4-Agness NICELY (NUSLI)
          (13 Nov 1841-19 Mar 1863)
. . . . .4-Isaac NICELY (NUSLI)
          (12 Oct 1843-21 Jun 1863)
. . . . .4-George A. NICELY (NUSLI) Jr.
          (1847-bef 1925)
. . . . .4-Hiram NICELY (NUSLI) (1849-bef 1929)
. . . . 3-Jacob NICELY (NUSLI) (abt 1810-abt 1892)
. . . . +Euphema UNKNOWN (abt 1811-bef 1901)
. . . . .4-John NICELY (NUSLI)
          (25 Jun 1837-29 Nov 1918)

. . . . 3-Martha NICELY (NUSLI) (1810-bef 1890)
. . . . +Charles NOEL (21 Oct 1808-1895)
. . . . .4-Shannon NOEL (29 Jul 1832-22 Dec 1910)
. . . . .4-George NOEL (13 Oct 1834-1906)
. . . . .4-Mary NOEL (13 Dec 1836-bef 1940)
. . . . .4-Tait NOEL (abt 1837-abt 1837)
. . . . .4-Unamed NOEL (abt 1838-abt 1838)
. . . . .4-Jonas NOEL (20 Sep 1839-3 Jul 1928)
. . . . .4-Elizabeth Marie NOEL
          (12 Sep 1842-25 Mar 1926)
. . . . .4-Margaret (Maggie) NOEL
          (12 Sep 1842-bef 1932)
. . . . .4-John C. NOEL (11 Nov 1845-19 Mar 1863)
. . . . .4-William NOEL (28 Sep 1848-26 Oct 1934)
. . . . .4-Sarah NOEL (11 Apr 1852-23 May 1935)
. . . . . +Esther SHIREY (SCHEIRY) (abt 1801-bef 1881)
. . . . 3-Susanna NICELY (NUSLI) (1822-bef 1902)
. . . . +Henry KIMMEL (1820-bef 1900)
. . . . .4-Mary KIMMEL (1842-bef 1932)
. . . . .4-Hester KIMMEL (1844-bef 1934)
. . . . .4-Susan KIMMEL (1846-bef 1936)
. . . . .4-Sarah Willa KIMMEL (1847-bef 1937)

. . . . .4-Tena E. KIMMEL (1849-bef 1939)

. . . . 3-Anthony A. NICELY (NUSLI)
             (26 Jun 1827-11 Jan 1908)

. . . . +Elizabeth JAMES (9 Dec 1827-9 Aug 1914)

. . . . .4-Josiah G. (Joseph) NICELY (NUSLI)
             (17 Feb 1849-2 Apr 1891)

. . . . .4-Daniel James NICELY (NUSLI)
             (30 Nov 1850-11 Nov 1896)

. . . . .4-Sarah (Sadie) NICELY (NUSLI)
             (4 Aug 1852-abt 1914)

. . . . .4-Amos NICELY (NUSLI)
             (23 Sep 1854-bef 1860)

. . . . .4-Ezra G. NICELY (NUSLI)
             (2 Oct 1856-1 Jan 1932)

. . . . .4-Elizabeth Amanda NICELY (NUSLI)
             (14 Apr 1858-abt 1914)

. . . . .4-Emmerretta NICELY (NUSLI)
             (26 Jan 1861-bef 1870)

. . . . .4-David Curtin NICELY (NUSLI)
             (1 Jan 1864-2 Apr 1891)

. . . . .4-Elenora (Ellen or Ella N.) NICELY
             (NUSLI) (28 Mar 1866-1936)

. . . . .4-Hettie Laura NICELY (NUSLI)
             (4 Jul 1868-1939)

. . . . 3-Catharine (Kathern) NICELY (NUSLI)
             (abt 1828-bef 1918)

. . . . +William MCKLVEEN (abt 1827-bef 1907)

. . . . .4-John E. MCKLVEEN
             (18 Jun 1847-31 Dec 1936)

. . . . 3-Philip NICELY (NUSLI)
             (9 Apr 1830-29 May 1866)

. . . . +Catharine SLATER (31 Dec 1831-23 May 1866)

. . . . .4-Sarah NICELY (NUSLI) (1855-bef 1935)

. . . . .4-Caroline NICELY (NUSLI) (1857-bef 1937)
. . . . .4-Araminta (Minta) NICELY (NUSLI)
   (12 Nov 1859-16 Mar 1941)
. . . . .4-Carrie Anna NICELY (NUSLI)
   (abt 1860-bef 1950)
. . . . .4-Leah Jane NICELY (NUSLI)
   (1856-bef 1946)
. . . . .4-W. Mack NICELY (NUSLI) (1862-bef 1930)
. . . . .4-Catherine Tate NICELY (NUSLI)
   (6 May 1866-21 Oct 1943)
. . . . 3-Louisa A. (Loweisanna) NICELY (NUSLI)
   (19 Aug 1832-13 Dec 1910)
. . . . +James C. AIKINS (14 Jul 1821-25 Dec 1906)
. . . . .4-Eliza Jane AIKINS (1850-bef 1940)
. . . . .4-John AIKINS (17 Mar 1851-19 Jun 1905)
. . . . .4-Ann AIKINS (1853-bef 1943)
. . . . .4-James W. AIKINS (Jul 1855-bef 1945)
. . . . .4-Rupert AIKINS (abt 1858-bef 1948)
. . . . .4-Louisa AIKINS (1858-bef 1948)
. . . . .4-Catharine AIKINS (abt 1859-bef 1950)
. . . . .4-Henry A. AIKINS
   (20 Dec 1860-3 Nov 1881)
. . . . .4-Albert G. AIKINS (1861-bef 1951)
. . . . .4-George Benjamine McCullan AIKINS
   (Aug 1862-5 Jun 1935)
. . . . .4-Mary AIKINS (1866-1956)
. . . . .4-May AIKINS (1868-bef 1958)
. . . . 3-William NICELY (NUSLI)
   (24 Jul 1834-25 Nov 1863)
. . . . +Maria TRUXAL (1833-bef 1925)
. . . . .4-Osborne NICELY (NUSLI)
   (abt 1859-bef 1939)
. . . . .4-Isaiah NICELY (NUSLI)
   (abt 1861-bef 1941)

. . . . 3-Henry (Heinrich) NICELY (NUSLI)
(23 Jun 1837-17 Nov 1863)
. . . . +Elizabeth TRUXAL (1836-Apr 1862)
. . . . .4-Emma L. NICELY (NUSLI)
(1859-5 Mar 1937)
. . . . .2-Mary Elizabeth (Polly) NICELY (NUSLI) (1765-1836)
. . . . . +Joseph (John) KARNS (KERUENS) (1755-1815)
. . . . .2-Catherine NICELY (NUSLI) (abt 1766-bef 1846)
. . . . . +John PIPER (abt 1765-bef 1845)
. . . . .2-Jacob (Tsu-Ka-We or Crow) NICELY (NUSLI)
(22 May 1770-1833)
. . . . . +Unknown UNKNOWN (WYNDOT INDIAN)
(abt 1786-bef 1866)
. . . . 3-Jacob (White Crow) WHITECROW (NUSLI)
(abt 1814-4 May 1876)
. . . . +Theresa BIG ARMS (1816-bef 1900)
. . . . .4-Jacob WHITECROW (NUSLI) Jr.
(10 May 1838-5 Sep 1885)
. . . . .4-Leander WHITECROW (NUSLI)
(1840-bef 1929)

. . . . .4-Betsy WHITECROW (NUSLI)
(1844-bef 1884)
. . . . .4-Mary Jane WHITECROW (NUSLI)
(1846-9 Dec 1878)
. . . . .4-Joseph WHITECROW (NUSLI)
(1848-3 Jan 1893)
. . . . .4-Sarah WHITECROW (NUSLI)
(1853-abt 1886)
. . . . .4-Lucinda (Lucy) WHITECROW (NUSLI)
(1853-31 Dec 1881)
. . . . 3-Jerry CROW (NUSLI) (abt 1815-22 Nov 1902)
. . . . +Unknown UNKNOWN (abt 1816-abt 1845)
. . . . .4-Lucy CROW (NUSLI) (abt 1836-bef 1926)

. . . . .4-Mary CROW (NUSLI) (abt 1838-bef 1928)
. . . . .4-Infant CROW (NUSLI) (abt 1840-bef 1930)
. . . . .4-Joseph CROW (NUSLI)
             (abt 1842-bef 1932)
. . . . +Koh-Wah-Sa-Ni-Ah UNKNOWN
          (abt 1824-13 Jan 1897)
. . . . . +Unknown SPICER (abt 1810-bef 1900)
. . . . . +Unknown UNKNOWN (abt 1786-bef 1866)
. . . . 3-Moses CROW (NUSLI) (abt 1817-abt 1861)
. . . . +Nancy UNKNOWN (1818-25 Dec 1896)
. . . . .4-William CROW (NUSLI)
             (abt 1838-abt 1863)
. . . . .4-Mary CROW (NUSLI) (abt 1840-abt 1868)
. . . . .4-Jane CROW (NUSLI) (abt 1852-3 Jun 1901)
. . . . .4-Amos CROW (NUSLI)
             (abt 1853-22 Apr 1904)
. . . . .4-John CROW (NUSLI) (1857-17 May 1931)
. . . . 3-Cah-Quee-Nah CROW (NUSLI)
          (abt 1818-bef 1903)
. . . . +Small Cloud SPICER (abt 1812-bef 1902)
. . . . .4-George SPICER (abt 1833-bef 1923)
. . . . .4-Joseph SPICER (1835-bef 1925)
. . . . .4-Daniel SPICER (1840-bef 1930)
. . . . .4-Armstrong SPICER (1843-bef 1933)
. . . . . +Unknown UNKNOWN (abt 1785-bef 1865)
. . . . 3-Wah-Deh-Dhyo-Do-Quah CROW (NUSLI)
          (abt 1819-bef 1895)
. . . . +John WINNEY (abt 1817-bef 1907)
. . . . .4-James WINNEY (abt 1840-12 Aug 1897)
. . . . .4-Isaac WINNEY (1849-28 Oct 1926)
. . . . .4-Lizzie WINNEY (abt 1850-bef 1932)
. . . . 3-Cah-Tee-Lih CROW (NUSLI)
          (abt 1821-bef 1890)
. . . . +John YOUNG (abt 1819-bef 1909)

.............4-Snow YOUNG (abt 1840-bef 1930)
.............4-Ko-He-Ta-Gay YOUNG
             (abt 1842-bef 1932)
.............4-Eliza YOUNG (abt 1844-bef 1934)
.....2-Margaretha (Margaret) NICELY (NUSLI)
             (10 Jun 1784-6 Sep 1854)
.....+John George AMBROSE (7 May 1778-11 Mar 1851)
.........3-Margaret AMBROSE (20 Dec 1804-24 Dec 1874)
.... +Jonathon BAKER (abt 1801-bef 1891)
........3-Frederick AMBROSE (abt 1805-abt 1860)
.... +Rosanna WEAVER (abt 1809-bef 1899)
.............4-Louise AMBROSE (24 Feb 1831-bef 1921)
.............4-Mary AMBROSE (19 Sep 1834-bef 1924)
.............4-Margaret AMBROSE
             (24 Feb 1836-bef 1926)
.............4-John AMBROSE (4 Dec 1837-17 Aug 1898)
.............4-William AMBROSE (17 Sep 1839-bef 1929)
.............4-Catherine AMBROSE (3 Jul 1842-1869)
.............4-David AMBROSE (24 May 1844-bef 1934)
.............4-Isaac AMBROSE (abt 1846-bef 1936)
.............4-Amos AMBROSE (abt 1848-bef 1938)
.............4-Lewis AMBROSE (abt 1850-bef 1940)
.............4-Hiram AMBROSE (Nov 1853-bef 1943)
........3-Elizabeth AMBROSE (abt 1806-bef 1885)
.... +Jacob HARGNETT (9 Nov 1805-25 Sep 1844)
.............4-Louvina HARGNETT
             (abt 1830-2 May 1899)
.............4-Lucy HARGNETT (abt 1832-1872)
.............4-Henry HARGNETT (abt 1836-bef 1926)
.............4-Sarah Jane HARGNETT
             (abt 1838-bef 1928)
.............4-Mary HARGNETT (abt 1843-bef 1933)
........3-Mary AMBROSE (14 Sep 1810-28 May 1882)
.... +John KELTZ (18 Mar 1809-7 Oct 1890)

. . . . .4-Alexander KELTZ (1835-bef 1915)
. . . . .4-Anthony KELTZ (6 Nov 1836-23 Dec 1890)
. . . . .4-Amanda KELTZ (1838-bef 1928)
. . . . .4-Adam KELTZ (abt 1838-bef 1928)
. . . . .4-Caroline KELTZ (abt 1840-bef 1930)
. . . . .4-Ellen KELTZ (abt 1844-bef 1934)
. . . . .4-Christena KELTZ
            (22 Apr 1847-2 Mar 1903)
. . . . .4-Mary KELTZ (Nov 1849-23 Aug 1923)
. . . . .4-Harriet KELTZ (abt 1856-bef 1946)
. . . . .4-John KELTZ (Oct 1852-abt 1877)
. . . . 3-Catherine AMBROSE (abt 1814-bef 1904)
. . . . +Gerhart LUTIS (abt 1813-bef 1903)
. . . . .4-Marie L. LUTIS (abt 1833-bef 1923)
. . . . .4-Annette L. LUTIS (abt 1836-bef 1926)
. . . . .4-Margaret Catherine LUTIS
            (abt 1838-bef 1842)
. . . . +Daniel KUHNS (abt 1795-bef 1885)
. . . . .4-John KUHNS (abt 1843-bef 1933)
. . . . .4-Elizabeth KUHNS (abt 1845-bef 1935)
. . . . .4-Mary K. KUHNS (abt 1845-bef 1850)
. . . . .4-Nancy S. KUHNS (abt 1848-bef 1850)
. . . . .4-Catherine KUHNS (abt 1850-bef 1940)
. . . . 3-Louise AMBROSE (5 Aug 1817-14 Mar 1849)
. . . . +Lewis BAUGHMAN (abt 1815-29 Sep 1895)
. . . . .4-Maria BAUGHMAN (abt 1840-bef 1930)
. . . . .4-Israel BAUGHMAN (abt 1842-1865)
. . . . .4-Lawrence BAUGHMAN
            (abt 1844-bef 1934)

. . . . .4-Margaret BAUGHMAN
            (abt 1845-bef 1935)
. . . . .4-Joseph BAUGHMAN (abt 1849-bef 1939)
. . . . 3-Sarah AMBROSE (29 Apr 1821-2 Apr 1849)

.... +Moses HEALEY (Dec 1826-6 May 1849)
..............4-Jonathan HEALEY (abt 1849-bef 1859)
.....2-Ann Elizabeth NICELY (NUSLI)
      (29 Oct 1786-bef 1866)
..... +Michael MILLER (abt 1795-bef 1875)

Ancestors of Adam NICELY (NUSLI) Sr.

Adam NICELY (NUSLI) Sr.: born in 1730 in East Hempfield Twp., PA, USA; died in 1826 in Original Nicely Farm, Donegal Twp., Westmoreland Co. PA, USA.

Parents:
Antonius Kristopher KNUSSLI (NUSLI) Sr.: born on 20 Sep 1657 in Eggiwil Bern, Canton of Switzerland; died on 14 May 1733 in Conestoga Manor, Hempfield Twp., Lancaster, PA, USA.
Elizabeth YEAGER: born about 1713; died before 1793.

Grandparents:
Hans KNUSSLI (NUSLI): born on 11 Oct 1628 in Zell, Zurick, Switzerland; married on 11 Jan 1650; died after 1688.
Elsbeth MULLER: born in ca. 1628; died in 1665.

APPENDIX C

Historical Accounts of the Events

Included in this appendix are the historical reports recorded in the various resources that were the basis for much of our research. I am including them since these publications are rare and not easy to locate. I am including only the sections that apply directly to our family information. Keep in mind that some of the information has proven to be inaccurate and the information in the chapters pertaining to each story has made note of these corrections.

Old & New Westmoreland History

Anthony Kneisle (as the name was originally spelled), came in 1730 from Hesse Darmstadt, Germany, landing in Philadelphia after a tedious voyage of six months. He was accompanied by his two brothers, Jacob and John, and also by Jacob Bergen and John Yeager, the two last-named bringing their families with them. Leaving Philadelphia the little company of immigrants traveled on foot to the southwestern part of Pennsylvania, settling in what was the Donegal Township, but is now part of Ligonier Township. It was about four miles west of Fort Ligonier, on the banks of the Four-Mile Run, that they found an abiding place. In the forest they constructed dwellings of logs, the house build by Adam Nicely being still in existence and the property of Colonel Anderson, of Latrobe, and Mrs. Mackey, of Ligonier. The Nicely brothers took up, among them, about twelve hundred acres, clearing a large part of this and planting corn. They carried their produce to Cumberland, Maryland, and purchased their salt at Saltsburg, Westmoreland County. They suffered frequently and severely from the aggressions of the Indians, the wife and two children of Jacob Nicely being slain by the savages. This so discouraged the unfortunate man that he left the neighborhood and is supposed to have gone to Armstrong County, where many of the names of Nicely claim a Jacob Nicely for their ancestor. Anthony and John Nicely remained in Westmoreland County, where some of their descendants are still to be found. A part of the original John Nicely tract is still in the family name and is owned by Joseph Nicely.

Anthony Nicely married Elizabeth, a sister of John Yeager, and their children were: Anthony, mentioned below; Adam; and some daughters who went West and whose names have not come down to us. The mother of the family died at the age of seventy years. All were members of the Lutheran church.

Anthony (2) Nicely, son of Anthony (1) and Elizabeth (Yeager) Nicely was born on the homestead which in the course of time he inherited. Of his six hundred acres he brought two hundred under cultivation, erecting barns and outbuildings, raising good stock and in all respects greatly improving the place. In politics, Mr. Nicely was a Whig and it is said of him that he never missed an election. The family was members of the Lutheran church. Mr. Nicely married --, and the following children were born to them: Anthony, married Rosanna Keltz; George, mentioned below; Eliza, twin to George, married John Ankerman; Adam, married Mary Best; and Elizabeth, married Sylvester Miller. At his death Mr. Nicely bequeathed to his descendants an estate, the value of which he had by his energetic and progressive management very materially augmented. He died in April 1845, at the age of eighty-four.

HISTORY OF WESTMORELAND COUNTY - ALBERT, George D., ed.: History of the County of Westmoreland, Pennsylvania, With Biographical

Sketches of Many of Its Prominent Men. Philadelphia: L. H. Everts & Co., 1882. CHAPTER XXIII - pgs. 115-118

We may also notice that Jacob Nicely, a little child, son of Adam Nicely, a resident on the Four-Mile Run not far from the Loyalhanna, was taken by a squad of those Seneca Indians, but at a time somewhat later, perhaps not earlier than 1791. He was watched by them when he was going from the house, where he had got a light-cake from his mother, to the other children, who were picking berries in the meadow. The children reported of his capture, and the party was followed beyond the Kiskiminetas, but without avail. He had been gone so long that he parents and their friends never expected even to hear of him. Jakey, as the people always spoke of him, was about five years old when taken. He was raised by them and adopted into the tribe. He forgot almost everything about the whites, and could not pronounce his own name when he had heard it. Many years after, when all was peace, a person from the valley, recognizing a similarity between the features and the build of this man and a brother, made inquiry, and found that he was an adopted white, and had been carried from Ligonier Valley. This was reported to the father, Adam Nicely, who after weeks of preparation started, about 1828, to see Jakey before he died, for he was now in old age. The mother, too, was still alive. The old gentleman made the journey in safety, and met and lodged with his boy, now to all intents an Indian. He had grown to manhood, and had a squaw for a wife, was raising a family, and had abundance of horses, some land, and plenty of hunting and fishing "tools." The old man returned, and "Jakey" promised him to come in the following year to see his mother. He gave his father a rifle for a keepsake, and accompanied him for some distance on his way back. Jakey did not come in as he promised, and they never heard more of him. When the father spoke of him, "his

Jakey," tears always filled his eyes. But the motherly yearning of the mother ceased for her idol of a boy only when they laid her whitened head on its earthly pillow to its last and sweetest sleep.

History of Westmoreland County, Volume 1, Chapter 7, Part 2 by John N. Boucher, New York, the Lewis Publishing Company, 1906.

Jacob Nicely was one of the last boys captured by the Indians in Westmoreland County. This took place in 1790, or perhaps a year later. The circumstances surrounding it are well authenticated. He was the son and perhaps the youngest son of Adam Nicely, who lived on the Four-Mile Run, about two miles from its junction with the Loyalhanna Creek.

One bright morning the Nicely children were out in the meadow picking berries, when the little boy Jacob started to the house. The mother was baking, and giving the child a warm cake, told it to rejoin the other children. But the child came back, saying the cake was too hot, and the others poured some cold water on it and again the child went away. These little journeys were closely watched by a party of Seneca Indians concealed near by. They captured the boy on his way back to the meadow. His capture, his struggles to free himself, and his cries, were seen and heard by the other children, who ran home and reported it to their parents. The father raised a company of willing neighbors who pursued the Indians with all possible speed. They traced them to the Kiskiminetas river, but in a wilderness beyond their track was soon lost. The father and his neighbors then returned to the heartbroken mother.

The captured boy was about five years old, and was at once adopted into the Seneca tribe. He rapidly forgot almost all he knew about his home and people in the lonely valley of the Loyalhanna. He readily acquired the habits and customs of the Indians, and was to all intents and purposes a member of the Seneca tribe. He learned to speak a new language, and forgot the few words taught him in childhood by his mother. He even forgot his own name, and could not pronounce it when he heard it. He spoke the Seneca language as though born in the wilderness, and spoke his mother tongue haltingly, as did his Indian associates.

Many years after, a trader, perhaps a fur dealer, who lived near the Nicely family on Four-Mile Run, chanced to be among the Senecas and saw this captive, now grown to manhood. The traveler was so impressed by the resemblance of the man to the Nicely family, whom he knew well in the Ligonier Valley, that he made inquiry, and learned that the man had been captured when a child in Westmoreland County. The traveler came home and reported this to the Nicely's in 1828, his mother had passed her three-score years and ten. A brother of the captured boy decided at once to visit the Indian tribe and see the long lost captive. Neighbors spoke dissuadingly of the project, but he was determined, and after a short preparation mounted a horse and rode away to the northern tribe. He made the journey in safety and found his brother. There was no doubt of the identity in the minds of either of them. The captured brother had been married to a squaw, and had around him a family of Indian children. He was prosperous for his surroundings, and had about him plenty of land, horses and cattle, and was well supplied with hunting and fishing implements. When his brother was in his house, he sent out to procure a white woman as cook, for the Indian manner of preparing meals was not supposed to be palatable to white people. There is a tradition in the family that the captured brother had visited Westmoreland prior to this, trying to locate his people and his home, and that, mispronouncing his name, he could not find them. At all events, Jacob arranged with his brother to visit his mother and relatives the following year. He also accompanied his brother part of the way home, made him a present of a rifle, etc. But the captive son and brother did not come as he promised. Perhaps he died before the following year, which was the time set for his visit. At all events, he was never heard from again. When the aged mother spoke of him, which was very often as the years advanced, she always called him her "Jakey" and with her eyes filled with tears. After a while the family ceased to look for him, but his mother never gave up the idea that he would return to her. Her hair grew gray in fruitless longing for a sight of her long lost child, and this yearning only ceased when her whitened head was pillowed in its last and sweetest sleep.

This is a small portion of a letter written by Famar Genevia McCurdy Copeland to her brother Oscar on August 30, 1888. The Ligonier Echo, as part of a handout, published this letter at a Fort Ligonier Day celebration in the 1970's.

Ligonier, Pennsylvania
August 30, 1888
Dear Brother Oscar;

........Another story happened about 100 years ago. There are many Nicely's in the Valley. Adam's son, Jacob, five years old, was captured by the Indians in the summer of 1790. He had gone with his brothers and sisters to pick berries. Jacob returned to get cookies and was captured on his way back. His father lost the trail at the Kiskiminetas River. In 1823, a man recognized Jacob, who had been adopted by the Senecca's in Warren County and had a family and considerable wealth and possessions. His father had died but his seventy-year-old mother sent Jacob's brother to see him.

Jacob had tried to find his family, but could not locate them not being able to pronounce the family name. Jacob gave his brother a rifle and other implements and returned part way, promising to return to the Valley, but never did they say.

The History of Wyandot County, Ohio, Leggett, Conaway and Company, Chicago, Illinois, 1884"

............Even in 1817 there were several captives among the Senecas and Wyandots, such as Spicer, Knisely, Sarah Williams, Mrs. Castleman, Eliza Whittaker, Sally Frost, Van Meter and others referred to in the History of Ohio. Those who were carried away in their youth were raised by Indian foster mothers, and became more Indian than the Indians themselves.....William Spicer, or Big Kittles, a captive of the Wyandots, was a native of Pennsylvania, made captive about 1775, and brought to the Ohio River, where the Wyandots would tie him to a tree near the river bank, so as to attract the attention of white travelers, who, on coming to release the boy, would themselves be captured. He moved to the Sandusky about 1778, grew up here, and became a large stock raiser and farmer. About 1821 he was beaten and then robbed of several thousand dollars, it is alleged, by a carpenter named Williams Rollins, an employee of P. D. Butler, at Fort Ball, in 1821. At that time Benjamin Barney and a constable named Papineau, a polished French-Canadian, and Caleb Rice espoused Spicer's cause, arrested Rollins, Downing, Butler and Case, brought them to trial, and had Rollins sentenced to eleven years in the penitentiary. A year later Spicer himself signed a petition asking pardon for the robber. A good deal of the $6,000 or $7,000 stolen was returned to this prosperous captive, who died here about 1830. One of his daughters was the second wife of Crow, another captive. Spicer's cabin, like himself, is said to have been the filthiest west of the

Alleghenies. This WILLIAM SPICER was charged in 1830, with the murder of Drake, the mail carrier, son of Judge Drake, of Marion County.....

CROW, OR JACOB KNISELY, was made captive in his youth by the Wyandots at Loyal Hannah, Pennsylvania, and carried to the Ohio River; thence brought to the Sandusky and transferred to the Senecas, with whom he moved West in 1831-32. He was made captive in 1778. Fifty years later his father came to Seneca County and stayed at Crow's cabin. The captive refused to answer any questions, until Mr. Knisely said: "If you are my son, then your name is Jacob." Crow responded enthusiastically saying: "That is my name and I am your son. I recollect that, but I kept it all to myself for fear that somebody would claim me and take me away." A very old Wyandot squaw, the woman who adopted young Knisely and named him Crow, was sent for to the Wyandot Reservation, and she confirmed the fact, but watched her foster son lest his father would induce him to return to civilization. In early years Crow married a Wyandot woman, who died, but before leaving for the West, he took William Spicer's daughter as his wife. He would not return with his father, parting with him forever at Bellevue. He died in 1833. White Crow, a son of Crow by his second wife, visited the old reservation here in 1852, after leaving his sons in school at Dayton. He is now known as Jacob Knisely. When here, he reported that the interpreter Herrin murdered Peter Pork on the Neosha.

History of Ohio, a chapter titled "History of Seneca County", "The Harris Family", pages 115, 116, 117, 118, 119

..."I knew all the Indians on the reserve, and was well acquainted with CROW. He was stolen by the Wyandots on the Loyal Hannah in Pennsylvania, and given to the Senecas, who adopted him. Crow was about two or three when he was taken away. The parents were away from home at the time and the other children out after berries. The savages got away with the child unobserved.

When Crow's father came to hunt him up, he stopped at Crow's and sent for my grandfather to come and interpret the conversation. Crow could not talk English. So I went along and heard all that was said. Mr. Jacob Knisely came on horseback to look for his son. He stated all about the manner of the stealing of his son, and said he had now visited all the lodges of the other tribes without success. My grandfather had been with the Senecas so much that he spoke their language quite fluently. He was one of the few who made their escape at the massacre of Wyoming.

They talked a long time. Crow did not want to talk: denied every recollection of his white ancestry, and often refused to give any answer. Finally Mr. Knisely said to him, "If you are my son, then your name is Jacob." With this, Crow jumped up and said, "That is my name, and I am your son; I recollect that, but I kept it all to myself for fear that somebody would claim me and take me away". Crow then sent up to the Wyandots and had his foster-mother come down, who corroborated Mr. Knisely' version of the stealing of his child. She was a very old squaw, and stayed several days, and as long as Mr. Knisely stayed, to satisfy herself that Crow would not go back with his father. Mr. Knisely tried every way to induce his son to go back with him to Pennsylvania; he said that his wife had been sick some time; that she had mourned for her lost child some fifty years, and would be willing to die if she could only once more see her dear boy. The scene was very affecting; but Crow was immovable. He said he had now a family of his own to look after and could not go, but promised to visit his parents some other time. He laughed heartily over the idea as to how he would look dressed up like a white man. Mr. Knisely left one morning, and Crow accompanied his father as far as Bellevue, where they stayed together all night. Crow returned next day, and when the Indians started for their new homes in the West he went with them. He never went to see his parents at all. Crow got his share of the treaties with the Wyandots, as well as with the Senecas, and become quite well off. Crow's first wife was a full blood Indian; his second wife was a daughter of William Spicer. White Crow was his oldest son, who came back here on a visit in 1852, and stayed with me one night. He had just then been at Dayton, Ohio, where he left his second son at school, and where his oldest son was also securing an education. Tears came into his eyes when he looked at the old reservation and he regretted that he had ever left. When the Senecas were paid off, Crow received for his improvements nine-hundred and fifty dollars, and another Indian paid him fifty dollars on an old debt. Martin Lane was an interpreter for the Senecas and went with them to the West, and returned here.... Col. McIlvain was the chief agent for the Senecas, and often stopped with Lane at the Spicer place. The Senecas were very slow getting ready to go. Finally they got their things on the wagons and started. Spicer was dead before they left here. Crow died at his new home of cholera. White Crow got rich, and adopted the name of his Grandfather Knisely.... Mr. Montgomery preached Spicer's funeral sermon. George Herrin, a half-Mohawk, was interpreter and gave the sermon in the Indian, sentence by sentence (slow preaching).... One of Spicer's boys, Small Cloud, was a fine looking fellow, a halfblood. He married CROW'S daughter by his first wife. Little Town Spicer has three or four wives. Both of these Spicer boys went West with the Senecas. CROW was a great deer hunter, and shot many a fine buck after night. He would then carry a pole seven feet long, pointed at the end, and with a fork at the upper end. A piece of bark, about fifteen inches wide and two feet long, was fastened to the fork so as to make the bottom level and the other end sticking up along the pole, like the letter L. A candle was put into the bottom part and CROW holding this over his head, was in the shade, but could see objects far off. The deer would look at the light and not notice CROW in the dark. As soon as CROW saw a deer, he would stick the pole in the soft ground, and make sure of his game. This was called "fire hunting", and CROW would always travel along the edge of the river, where the deer would come down to drink and find "salt licks".

Note

As I noted in one of the earlier chapters, the Westmoreland County History Books can be viewed on the Internet at pa-roots.com under the Pennsylvania, Westmoreland County section. A large number of the chapters have been converted and some are still under conversion.

APPENDIX D

Travel Directions around Four-Mile Run

If you would like to take a tour around the area covered in this book, following are directions including mileage information based on traveling on Route US 30.

1. Head west on Route US 30 from Ligonier; turn left at the top of the hill just past Timberlink Golf Course and Idlewild Park. If you traveling on Route US 30 east from Latrobe, after you across Longbridge and crest the top of the hill, turn right. Check your odometer mileage as you make this turn.

2. Go 0.35 mile to a stop sign. Turn left.

3. Go 1.65 miles and the Keltz Cemetery is on the right. Most of the early family members are buried in this cemetery. Parking is difficult here so you might want to park a short distance up the road near the fire station and walk back. If you turn around one car has room to park partway off the road on the right side. Please be careful of the traffic here.

4. From the front of the Keltz Cemetery, Go 0.5 mile to Hidden Valley Road on the right. YOU MIGHT WANT TO SKIP THIS SECTION OF THE TRIP. This side trip takes you to Fuller Nicely Hollow. The road up through this hollow was the wagon road the Nicely family used to reach their home when they moved to the area in the 1760's and for many years later. The road comes to a dead-end now and once you reach the end, you must turn and come back out. IF YOU DECIDE TO SKIP THIS TRIP GO TO STEP 8.

If you decide to take this side trip turn into Hidden Valley Road (NO OUTLET) please drive slowly especially at turns and crests of hills. This road is very narrow and if you meet someone it will require one of you to back up to a convenient passing spot.

5. At 0.6 mile, keep going straight. A Private road goes to the left.

6. At 0.2 mile after coming around a sharp bend there is a house setting back in the field to the left. Back near the stream to the left of the house, it is believed was the location of the Fuller Stage stop. At this time you are now heading up the Fuller Nicely Hollow. So named because the property ended up being owned by Fuller John Nicely a descendant of Adam Nicely Sr. At this point, you are now in the approximate area of the original road to the farm. The Forbes Road was also near this area and in fact this may have been the Forbes Road.

7. Go 0.3 mile. This is the end of the road. The entrance to the original Nicely farm is about ½ to ¾th of a mile farther up past the roadblock. The road to the farm turned to the left at this point and climbs the hill to the homestead. This road was closed several years ago and originally went up over the hill and then met up with the current Darlington to Youngstown road. Later on you will reach the original farm site from the opposite side of the farm. Turn around at this point and travel back to the main road. Again be careful in returning on this road. As you reach the main road at the end of Hidden Valley Road, check your mileage again and turn right.

8. Go 0.3 mile. On the left was where they took their wagons up through the hollow over the ridge on the way to

Ligonier. The wagon trail was part of the original Forbes Road and goes down the other side of the ridge in front of the Urch Farm, where an original log home still stands. This log house belonged to one of my boyhood friends and I stayed overnight at this house on many occasions. The wagon trail continued past the house in a straight line through where the barn is currently located and crossed over the ridge behind the barn and continued to the current Route 711 before heading into Ligonier.

9. Go 0.7 mile. The road you are traveling on, before you reach the 0.7 mileage mark, is just to the right of where the old wagon road was located. The Nicely's and others used this wagon road as they traveled to Ligonier and back to the farm. The stream to your right is Four-Mile Run. At the 0.7-mile mark on your odometer you will see on the right a bend in the Four-Mile Run. This is the place where they forded the Four-Mile Run to go up through the Fuller Nicely Hollow that you were on earlier. You will notice an old concrete bridge abutment on the left side of the stream. A bridge was built there probably in the late 1800's and was used in place of fording the stream. Just across the run is the most likely area where the Wyandot Indians came down the hill from the farm carrying Jacob as they began their escape down Four-Mile Run. They had probably traveled downstream along the stream that was created by the spring behind the original log home until they reached the Four-Mile Run.

10. Go 0.3 mile. Turn right at the fork in the road. The hill on the left fork is Fairveiw Hill. You will return to this place later and go up Fairveiw Hill.

11. Go 0.2 mile. As you cross the bridge over the Four-Mile Run, you are now on a part of the original 1200-acre Nicely land grant. The property line went off to the right along the stream bank in one direction and crossed up over the Fairveiw Hill on your left. At this point in time I am not sure where all the lines were located, but it did extend from this point up over the hill to the left towards the Ligonier Country Club Golf Course and to right of this bridge to the top of the Chestnut Ridge.

12. Go 0.2 mile. George Allen Brown (G.A.B.) Nicely had the barn and the older farmhouse just past the barn constructed in approximately 1881. He built this house and barn for his wife who wanted to move closer to town, but they never lived in it. She was not happy with the new place and wanted to move to Ligonier. He sold this farm and the original farm in 1905 in two separate parcels.

13. After you pass the farmhouse, go 1.25 miles. As you drive you can see the Four-Mile Run to your left. Turn to the right at the 1.25-mile mark. It's easy to drive past this road so be alert.

14. Go 0.3 mile. Turn right. This was the new entrance created sometime in the early 1800's into the Nicely homestead. Keep going straight. There is a gate now across the road. The house and barn are being renovated and entrance is by permission only. The barn and farmhouse are a short distance from the gate. Gene Pluto, a descendant of Anthony Nicely, purchased this land in December 2003. The farmhouse standing there is the original house that was built by Anthony Nicely in 1810. The barn standing there now was reconstructed after a fire burned the original barn to the ground. The stone

foundation under the barn is the original barn foundation. This house stands on the property where the Wyandot Indians captured Jacob in 1775. The capture took place about ½ mile past the farmhouse. The original log house location is along the old township road, which extends straight out across the field. You can see the remains of the cut in the land for this old road. This road is not passable by car, so in order to see the homesite you must walk. Please contact the author or Gene Pluto before making this walk. The log house was located about ½ mile straight ahead on the right side of the road on the opposite side of the hill you see directly ahead of you. The house, on the left, was not standing at the time of the capture and the fields you see ahead of you were not cleared at that time. The home site location is difficult top see due to the undergrowth and will require someone to take you there. There is a section of ground with a leveled area that is approximately 18 feet by 22 feet, which would be large enough to accommodate a log home in 1761. It is about 10 feet off the cut of the old road on the right side. There is evidence of dirt removed on the upper side of the slope to allow this leveling. There is also a spring down over the hill from the home site with stones still buried in the bank that appear to be the original lean to probably built by Adam Sr. in 1761. In 2007, Sid and Leora Whitecrow made a visit and a group of family members went with us to see this location. While moving down the hill to the springhouse area, Jake Knisely and Leora were walking together and a black crow feather was lying on the ground in Leora's path. She picked it up, closed her eyes and said little Jakey told me this is where the capture took place. It was a very emotional moment. There were probably berry patches located all around the area, so it's difficult to say where the children may have been picking berries. From the place where the feather was found is was only a short distance to where the spring stream and the old farm road ran down to the Four Mile Run. The Indians carrying Jacob would have followed the old farm road and the stream created by the spring down the hill below the home site through the hollow and to the Four-Mile Run below.

15. When you leave the farm back track along the Four-Mile Run the same direction you came in and continue about 2.5 miles until you cross over Four-Mile Run on the bridge and come to the stop sign. Turn right up Fairview Hill.

16. Go 1.4 miles. Most of the road you are now on was part of the original farm. Consider that 1,200 acres would be a piece of ground approximately 5/8 of mile wide by 3 miles long. Turn left on Zion Church road. At 0.2 mile on the left is the Zion Church and on the right is a cemetery. This is the Zion Church Cemetery. There is only one Nicely headstone in this cemetery. Henry Nicely born June 22, 1837 and died Nov 17, 1863. He was the youngest son of Adam and Esther Shirey Nicely Jr. However this church was built on Anthony A. Nicely's land and he was part of the group who built the church. The church was named the Nicely Church of the Brethren for a number of years after it was constructed in 1874. It is now named the Zion Church.

17. Turn at the cemetery and come back 0.2 mile to the stop sign and turn left.

18. Go 0.4 mile. Turn left. You are still on part of the original Nicely farm. Members of the Nicely family originally farmed many of the properties on both sides of this road.

19. Go 0.65 mile. The road on the left that is marked Private Road, Rolling Rock leads to the original farm site that was established by Adam Nicely Jr. when he left the original home site and the farm was split into two farms. Adam Jr. built the barn and house in ca. 1800. The home was a log house, but the log portion is now enclosed by expansion of the home over the years. This is the first farm on the right side of the road as you go down the hill.

20. As you turn and come back out, turn left.

21. Go 0.35 mile and turn left towards Ligonier.

22. Go 2.4 miles and on left your will see Nicely Road and the Ligonier Valley Cemetery. You can turn up into the cemetery where many of the Nicely gravesites are located. If you follow Nicely Road for about 0.4 mile you will see a swinging bridge across the Loyalhanna Creek on the right and on the left you will see the farmhouse that G.A.B. Nicely bought when he moved off of the original Nicely homestead. It has been remodeled in 2010 and is encased in brick. The original exterior was wood.

23. I hope this helps you find your way around the area.

The following aerial view will assist you in finding your way around the area of the Anthony Nicely 1810 farm.

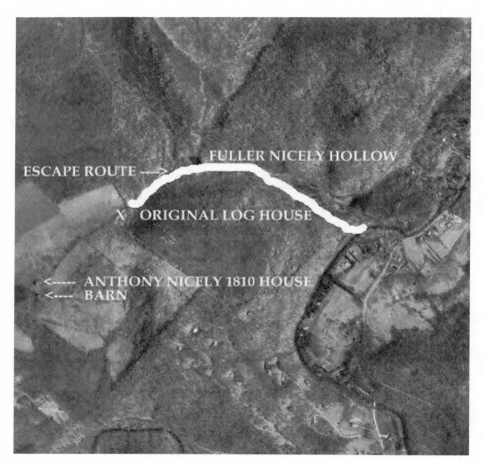

APPENDIX E

Family Wills

Following are the wills of the two sons Anthony and Adam Jr. who each inherited 600 acres of the original Adam Kneisle homestead.

Anthony Nicely Sr.'s Last Will and Testament

In the name of God Amen. I Anthony Nicely Sr. of Ligonier Township, Westmoreland County and State of Pennsylvania, being somewhat indisposed in body, but being of sound mind and memory do make and publish this my last will and testament in manner and form following viz. First I give and bequeath to my beloved wife Sarah Nicely the occupancy of the house wherin my son George now resides during her natural life, likewise a garden and sufficiency of firewood ready cut at the door, also I give and bequeath a Horse Creature and a Cow such as she may choose out of the flock together with a bed and saddle and bridle, together with household and kitchen furniture in the amount of thirty dollars. - Item I give and bequeath to the eldest son Anthony Nicely, the tract of land formerly owned by my father wherever he now resides as his heirs and assigns forever, likewise the legacy coming to me from George Eager's Estate. My son Anthony is to pay my son Adam one hundred dollars, to be paid in the following manner viz. twenty five dollars one year after my decease and twenty five dollars annually till the whole is paid. Item I give and bequeath to my son Adam Nicely the farm whereon he now resides the boundary as formerly chained by John Carns together with the piece of land which I bought of John Shale, to him his heirs and assigns forever. Item I give and bequeath to my son George Nicely the farm whereon I now reside his heirs and assigns forever my son George to pay to my son Adam One hundred dollars to be paid as follows fifty dollars one year after my decease and fifty dollars two years after my decease and furnish his mother with the necessaries of life, wood is included. Item I give and bequeath to my daughter Mary Aukerman five hundred dollars in cash. Item I give and bequeath to my daughter Elizabeth Miller two hundred dollars in cash. It is my will that my movable property be sold and an equal division of the ___ be made among all my children. I hereby appoint my son Anthony Nicely and John Aukerman Executors of this my last will and testament revoking all former wills by me made. In witness whereof I have set my hand and seal this fifth day of February one thousand eight hundred and forty five.

Anthony Nicely, Sr.

Signed, sealed, published and declared by the above named Anthony Nicely, Sr. to be his last will and testament in the presence of us who at his request and in his presence have subscribed our names as witnesses thereunto. Legally proved and approved the 8th and 11th days of December, A. D. 1845. Same day recorded and Letters Testamentary granted to Executors. Samuel Keltz, John Nicely, Executors sworn before D. Cook, Reg'r

Adam Nicely Jr.'s Last Will and Testament

In the name of God Amen. I, Adam Nicely of the township of Ligonier in the county of Westmoreland and State of Pennsylvania ___ being weak in body and of sound mind and memory and understanding but considering the uncertainty of this transitory life do make and publish this last will and testament in manner of the following, to wit. First it is my will and I do order that all of my just debts and funeral expenses be duly paid and satisfied as soon as conveniently can be after my decease. Item. I give and do bequeath unto my dear wife Esther the use of the plantation or farm on which I now reside so long as she remains my widow or until my youngest son arrives at the age of twenty-one years. Also whatever horses, cows, sheep, hogs, farming utensils, households and kitchen furniture as may be considered necessary for my said widow to farm the premises and support my minor children. She my said widow to educate them out of the proceeds of said farm - Item. I give and bequeath unto my eight eldest children to wit, Adam Nicely III, Elizabeth Nicely married to Peter Miller, John Nicely, Margaret Nicely, married to Shannon Roberts, George Nicely, Rosanna Nicely married to Alexander McDowell, Martha Nicely married to Charles Noel and Jacob Nicely the sum of twenty five dollars each to be paid to them one year after my decease which __ I do hearby declare to be in lieu and stead of this ___ at law. Item. I give and bequeath unto my younger children to wit, Anthony, Philip and William, the plantation or farm on which I reside to be for them, their heirs and ___ forever they maintaining and supporting my said wife Esther during her natural life or so long as she remains my widow. In case my said widow should again marry she is to have as such property for her own use as the laws of the Commonwealth of Pennsylvania now allow to insolvent debtors. Item. I give and bequeath to my children Anthony, Philip, William, Catherine, Susanna and Louisa all the rest and remainder of my estate real and personal of what kind and nature __ the same may be in the county of Westmoreland or elsewhere to be equally divided among them. And further in case there should be any further progeny or offspring the same if a son shall be entered to and receive an equal proportion of any estate all real and personal the same as the last three named sons and if a daughter the same proportion as the last three named daughters and if either should depart this life before they arrive at the age of twenty one years their proportion of said dower to be equally distributed amongst the above last named younger children. I also order and direct that my executor hereinafter named or the survivors of them shall have full power and authority to sell and dispose of any plantation purchases of ____ and to sign, seal, execute and acknowledge such deed or deeds of conveyance as shall or may be necessary for the granting or ____ the same to the purchasers thereof and the moneys arising therefrom to be put in the hands of such person and under such security as the laws of Pennsylvania approve for the [next line lost] at common law. And lastly I nominate and constitute and appoint my said wife Esther and James McKelvey esquire to be the executors of this my last will and testament hereby revoking all other wills, legacies and bequests by me heretofore made and declaring this and no other to be my last will and testament. In witness whereof I have hereunto set my hand and seal the twenty-seventh day of April AD one thousand eight hundred and thirty eight (1838).

Adam Nicely (in German)

Signed, sealed and declared by the said testator within names as his last will and testament in the presence of us – George Ambrose, Henry Brant

Legally proved and approved this 25th day of May AD 1838 – Same day recorded and Letters Testamentary ____ to Executors. Executors sworn____ ____ Row, Reg'r.

APPENDIX F

Surnames

The following list of 1,306 surnames represents a list of descendents of Adam and Elizabeth Eichert Kneisle Sr. who established his homesite in Ligonier, PA in 1761. These names have been currently documented in my research. This is not a complete list since all branches have not been traced to the current generation level. There are currently 3,325 blood descendents in my file as of today. I am still actively pursuing other branch information, which could lead to an increase in this number.

ACERINE	ARCHAMBEAULT	BAIRD
ACERNIE	ARMEL	BAKER
ACHHAMMER	ARMOR	BALDONI
ADAMKOVICK	ARMOUR	BALDWIN
ADAMS	ARMSTRONG	BALL
ADAMSON	ARTIM	BALLARD
AIKENS	ARTMAN	BALTHASER
AIKINS	ASBURY	BARBER
ALBOUGH	ASHBAUGH	BARKAN
ALBRIGHT	ASKINS	BARKLEY
ALCANTARA	ASSOLONE	BARNES
ALCANTORA	ASTIN	BARNEY
ALEX	ATKISON	BARNHARD
ALEXANDER	AUGUSTINE	BARNHART
ALLBOUGH	AUKERMAN	BAROTA
ALLER	(ACKERMAN)	BARRON
ALLISON	AUMAN	BARTON
ALLSHOUSE	AUSES	BASSETT
ALMES	AUSTIN	BATES
AMANTEA	AUSTRAW	BATTISTA
AMBROSE	AYLES	BAUGHMAN
ANDREYO	AZNAVORIAN	BAUM
ANKNEY	AZULE	BAUMAN
ANSARI	BABINSACK	BEAL
ANTE	BACHER	BEAM
ANTHONY	BAIR	BEARD

BEARFIELD	BOGGIO	BUTTERFIELD
BEARSKIN	BOLLINGER	BYERLY
BEASON	BOMBERRY	BYERS
BECER	BONDY	CABLE
BECK	BOOHER	CAIRNS
BEEBE	BOON	CALDWELL
BEER	BOOTH	CALHOUN
BELL	BORGO	CAMERON
BELLA	BORING	CAMPBELL
BELLAN	BORTZ	CAPELLA
BELLIS	BOUCHARD	CAPORALI
BELMONT	BOWERSOX	CARALLA
BELOVICH	BOYD	CARDOZA
BENDER	BRADICK	CARLESON
BENETIS	BRADLEY	CARLSON
BENNETT	BRANT	CARMEL
BENSON	BRANT (BRANDT)	CARNAHAN
BENTLEY	BRATHOVICS	CARNERA
BENZ	BRAUCHER	CARNS
BERGER	BRAUMBAUGH	CASEY
BERGSTROM	BRENNER	CASPER
BERNARD	BRESSWOOD	CASSADY
BERQUIST	BRIDGE	CASSEL
BERTOLET	BRINKER	CASTELLANI
BEST	BRISCOE	CASTNER
BETZ	BRODY	CASTON
BICE	BRONSON	CAWOSKI
BIER	BROSKY	CERUTTI
BIG ARMS	BROWN	CESTELLO
BILINSKI	BRUCE	CHAFFIN
BILLMAN	BRUINER	CHAMBERS
BILLS	BRUNER	CHAPMAN
BINKEY	BRUNNER	CHAPPELL
BIRCH	BRUNOT	CHARLES
BIRDWELL	BUELL	CHARLOE
BIRGAM	BUFFALIN	CHARLTON
BIRT	BURGAN	CHECKEYE
BITNER	BURKE	CHIEIK
BJORKLAND	BURKETT	CHITTENDEN
BLACKBURN	BURKHOLDER	CHOTEAU
BLACKWELL	BURLEY	CHOUTEAU
BLAIR	BURNS	CHRISLER
BLEVINS	BURRIS	CHRONOWSKI
BLOOM	BURRISS	CLAAR
BODNAR	BURZYNSKI	CLARK
BOGARD	BUTLER	CLAWSON

CLAY
CLAYPOOL
CLIFFORD
CLIM
CLINE
CLOPP
COBURN
COCHRAN
COFFMAN
COGAN
COLBERG
COLE
COLEMAN
COLLELL
COLLETTS
COLT
COMNALE
COMP
CONDRICK
CONDRON
CONNER
CONNERS
CONRAD
CONRATH
CONSIDINE
COOK
COOLEY
COOMBS
COON (KUHN)
CORBETT
CORLE
CORMAN
CORSI
COTTON
COTTONWOOD
COUGHENOR
COUNTRYMAN
(GUNDERMAN)
COX
COY
COZINE
CRAIG
CRANDALL
CRAVER
CRAWFISH
CRAWFORD

CRITCHFIELD
CROSBY
CROUSHORE
CROW (NUSLI)
CROWE
CULLEITON
CULLEN
CUMMINGS
CUNNINGHAM
CURTIS
CUSTY
CUTHBERT
CZARNESKI
D'AMORE
DAILEY
DANDO
DANKENSRIETER
DANKO
DANKS
DANO
DARR
DAVIES
DAVIS
DEAL
DEAN
DEANGELO
DEARMENT
DEEDS
DEERING
DEFFIBAUGH
DEIULIUS
DEMMITT
DENSTAEDT
DEPPEN
DERBY
DERSCH
DICESERE
DICK
DICKEY
DIGIOVANNI
DISNEY
DIXON
DOCKERY
DODDS
DODSON
DOMKA

DONAHUE
DONNALLEN
DONOVAN
DORAN
DORKA
DORMAN
DOTY
DOUBLE
DOUGHTY
DOUGLASS
DOUPLE
DRAKE
DREXLER
DUBICH
DUBICK
DUCKER
DUMAS
DUMNICH
DUNBAR
DUNLAP
DUNN
DUSTEN
DWYER
DYER
DYNKOWSKI
DYSARD
DZIEDZIC
EACUS
EASLICK
EDINBORO
EDMONDS
EISAMAN
ELBY
ELDER
ELLENBERGER
ELLIOT
ELLIOTT
EMCH
ENDERSBE
ENOS
ENYART
ERICKSON
ESKUT
ESTONTE
ETTER
ETTINGER

EVANS
EVERETT
EWING
EZYKOWSKY
FABEC
FABIAN
FAIT
FALBO
FALK
FARR
FARSTAD
FASTNACHT
FEE
FELBAUM
FELLO
FENNELL
FERNANDES
FERRY
FETTER
FEZARD
FILLMAN
FINNISH
FISCHER
FISH
FISHEL
FISHER
FIX
FLACK
FLECKENSTEIN
FLEMING
FLETCHER
FLIGGER
FLOCK
FOJTIK
FORCE
FORD
FOREMAN
FORSHA
FORSYTHE
FOUST
FOWLER
FOX
FRABLE
FRANCIS
FRANKLIN
FREDERICK

FREED
FREEMAN
FRITZ
FROST
FRY
FRYE
FULLERTON
FUMO
FURGESON
(FERGUSON)
GALBRAITH
GAMBLE
GARAVATT
GARCIA
GARRETT
GARRIS
GARTNER
GASKILL
GASKIN
GAYLEY
GEARING
GEER
GEETING
GELVIN
GENSAMER
GEORGE
GERLACH
GETTEMY
GIAMARCO
GIBSON
GILBERT
GILLAM
GILLIGAN
GILLILAND
GILLIS
GILMER
GILMORE
GINDLESBERGER
GIRARD
GLENDENNINS
GLENDINNINGS
GOLDBERG
GOODIN
GOODLIN
GORDAN
GRACE

GRAFF
GRAHAM
GRAMMER
(GRANER)
GRAY
GREATHOUSE
GREENAWAY
GREENLAND
GREENWOOD
GRIFFIN
GRIGER
GRIMM
GROSS
GROSZEWSKI
GROTE
GROTT
GROUNDS
GROVE
GRUSZCZYNSKI
GUISEPPINA
GULLIKSON
GUMBERT
GURSS
GUTHRIE
GUTIERREZ
GYAMI
HALL
HALNELT
HALZWORTH
HAM
HAMILL
HANK
HANKINSON
HANNA
HAPP
HARDING
HARDY
HARGNETT
HARKLEREAD
HARKNESS
HARR
HARRINGTON
HARRIS
HARTMAN
HASKELL
HAT

HATCH	HOLLOWAY	JACKSON
HAUCH	HOLSAPPLE	JACOBER
HAUGER	HOLTGREWE	JACOBY (JAMES)
HAUSER	HOLZER	JADRIK
HAUVER	HONE	JAMES
HAWK	HONS	JAMESON
HAYES	HOON	JAMIESON
HAYS	HOOPES	JAMISON
HAYSS	HOOVER	JANCZALAK
HEALEY	HOPKINS	JARMIC
HEARN	HORNING	JENKINS
HEBENTHAL	HOSACK	JENNINGS
HEBERT	HOUGH	JESSEE
HEETER	HOUPT	JOHNS
HEFFELMAN	HOUSEBERG	JOHNSON
HEIDE	HOUSER	JOHNSTON
HEIDORN	HOWELL	JONES
HEINTZELMAN	HREHOCIK	JONESHUTT
HELMICK	HUDWORTH	JORDAN
HELMSTADTER	HUEBNER	JOSEPH
HEMING	HUGHES	KABANA
HEMPHILL	HUGHS	KAHL
HENDERSON	HUGO	KAHRS
HENRY	HULL	KAPLAN
HENSLEY	HUMBLE	KAPUSTIK
HERMINZEK	HUMBLE-DYER	KARASAK
HESS	HUNT	KARIHO
HETRICK	HUNTER	(KAYRAHOO)
HIBERG	HURITE	KARNS
HICKS	HUSKA	KARNS (KERN)
HILL	HUSSY	KARNS (KERNS)
HIMES	HUSTON	KARNS (KERUENS)
HIND	HUTCHESON	KASSIMER
HINES	HUTCHINSON	KASTNER
HINMAN	HUTCHISON	KATCHUR
HINSON	HUTTENHOWER	KATLIC
HITCHMAN	HUTTON	KAYRAHOO
HLAVSA	HYDE	KAZALIA
HOBYAN	IAMS	KEAN
HOFECKER	ICKES	KEBERT
HOFFER	IDEMILLER	KEELER
HOGUE	IRVINE	KEENE
HOHO	IRWIN	KEGG
HOLDEN	ISLES	KEHL
HOLLAND	IWANIN	KEIM
HOLLICK	JACK	KELLER

KELLS	KRUNSZYKINSKY	LLOYD
KELLY	KUHNS	LOCHRIE
KELTZ	KUNKLE	LOFLAND
KEMP	KURTZ	LONG
KENLY	KUTZMILLER	LOOMAN
KENNEDY	LACIE	LOVE
KENT	LAEVESQUE	LOWMAN
KEOUGH	LAFERTY	LOWRY
KERR	LAFONTAINE	LUBECKI
KESTNER	LAMBERT	LUCKETT
KETO	LANE	LUFF
KETTERING	LANG	LUFT
KEYS	LARGE	LUND
KEYSER	LARIMER	LUTE
KIMES	LARUE	LUTHER
KIMMEL	LATERNEAU	LUTIS
KING	LAUDER	LYDIC
KINGFISHER	LAVELLE	LYNCH
KINSEY	LAWSON	LYNN
KINTZ	LAYCOCK	LYONS
KINZEY	LE GOSS	MACKEY
KIRBY	LEACH	MADAK
KIRCHNER	LEAR	MAHONE
KLEIN	LEARN	MANONE
KLINE	LEDBETTER	MARCINIK
KNAUF	LEE	MARIJKE
KNEE	LEFF	MARION
KNOPFEL	LEICHLITER	MARKER
KNOX	LEKSELL	MARKOVIC
KNUPP	LELAND	MARKS
KOHLER	LENHART	MARSH
KOLTER	LENTZ	MARSHALL
KONDEK	LEONARD	MARTIN
KOON	LEONARD	MASON
KOONTZ	(KUNKLE)	MASSA
KORPI	LESNEY	MASSIMINO
KOUGH	LESTITIAN	MATESIC
KOZEMCHAK	LEVAN	MATHEWS
KOZENKO	LEVELLE	MATSON
KRAL	LEVIS	MATTHEWS
KRAMER	LEWIS	MAY
KRINOCK	LINSENMAYER	MAYOR
KROMER	LISBON	MAZICK
KROMPEGAL	LISCH	MCBRIDE
KRONENBURG	LISTER	MCBROOM
KROZEK	LIVENGOOD	MCBURNEY

MCCACHRAN	METRO	MUSSATTO
MCCARTHY	METZGER	MYERS
MCCHESNEY	MEYER	NACE
MCCLAIN	MICKESELL	NAUGLE
MCCLEARY	MIEDEL	NEAL
MCCLENDON	MILBURN	NEIDERHISER
MCCLINTOCK	MILLAGE	NEILSON
MCCONNELL	MILLER	NELMS
MCCORMACK	MILLETTE	NELSON
MCCOY	MILLIGAN	NESS
MCCRACKEN	MILNER	NEWSOM
MCCREERY	MIMNA	NICELY (NUSLI)
MCDONNELL	MINEMYER	NICHOLS
MCDONOUGH	MINICK	NICKELSON
MCDOWELL	MINTO	NIEZELSKI
MCDOWELL (PIPER	MITCHEL	NIMMS
MCDOWELL)	MITCHELL	NOEL
MCFADDEN	MIX	NONOELLE
MCFARLAND	MOFFAT	NORRIS
MCGILL	MONSOUR	NULL
MCGINNIS	MONTALERO	NYLAND
MCHARGE	MONTANO	OATMAN
MCHENRY	MONTICUE	OLCZAK
MCINTIRE	MONTNEY	OLLIS
MCINTYRE	MOODY	OLUSZAK
MCKELVEY	MOORE	ONEIL
MCKENNA	MOORMAN	OROSZ
MCKENZIE	MORALES	ORR
MCKLVEEN	MOREHOUSE	OVERLY
MCLAIN	MORETTI	OWENS
MCLEOD	MORGAN	PACKER
MCLINDEN	MORRIS	PAIGE
MCMASTER	MORRISON	PAINTER
MCMILLEN	MORROW	PARK
MCWILLIAMS	MORTIMER	PARKER
MEEKER	MOSHOLDER	PARTLOW
MEHALCIC	MOSS	PASSEWITZ
MEISINGER	MOYHER	PATERSON
MELHORN	MUDD	PATTERSON
MELLOTT	MUELLER	PAUL
MELVILLE	MULL	PAUNOVICH
MENARCHIK	MULLEN	PAVARNIK
MENOHER	MULLIGAN	PAVLOVCAK
MENSCH	MUMFORD	PEACOCK
MERZ	MURPHY	PEARCE
MESMER	MUSH	PEASE

PECHNER	QUEER	ROLON
PECKART	QUIGG	ROMAN
PEFFER	QUINN	ROMIG
PELKEY	RAIMONDO	ROSCAMP
PENNEY	RAINBOLT	ROSE
PENNY	RALSTON	ROSS
PENROD	RAMAGE	ROSSER
PEOPLES	RAMSEY	ROWAN
PERKY	RAPPUIE	ROWE
PERRATONE	RATTI	ROWLAND
PERRY	RAUCH	ROYER
PERSHING	RAY	RUDY
PETERS	REA	RUFFINO
PETERSON	RECTOR	RULLO
PETRICK	REDMOND	RUMMELL
PETRITAS	REED	RUPP
PETROSKY	REEFER	RUSHER
PEWITT	REEPING	RYAN
PFANENSTIEL	REESE	RYNCOSKY
PFOUTZ	REHM	SABBERS
PHILLIPS	REICHLE	SALANDRO
PICK	RENNICK	SALAS
PIERCE	RENNINGER	SALYARDS
PIERZYNSKI	REPKO	SAMMS
PINKERTON	RHOADES	SANDERSON
PINNEY	RHODES	SARVEY
PIPER	RIBBLETT	SASKIEWICZ
PITKAVISH	RICE	SATTERLY
PLOWMAN	RICHWINE	SATZLER
PLUDE	RIDDELL	SAUCIER
PLUMMER	RIDDLE	SAYLOR
PLUTO	RIDER	SCANLON
PLYMIRE	RIFFLE	SCHAEFFER
POLLOCK	RIGGS	SCHANDEL
POORMAN	RIGNEY	SCHEURER
PORCH	RILEY	(SHIREY)
POSZ	RISHEBARGER	SCHIFFBAUER
POTEETE	RISHER	SCHILBERZ
POUNDS	ROADMAN	SCHMIDT
POWELL	ROBB	SCHOBER
PRICE	ROBERTS	SCHOPP
PRIDDY	RODDY	SCHRIBUER
PULLIAM	RODIBAUGH	SCHROEDER
PUSHINSKY	ROEHRIG	SCHUUR
PUTNAM	ROGERS	SCHUYLER
QUEENEY	ROHN	SCOTT

SCRITCHFIELD
SEALES
SEATON
SEBOLD
SEEMILLER
SELLERS
SENOR
SENSENIG
SEPTER
SERENA
SESONSKY
SESSI
SHABELLA
SHADRON
SHAEFFER
SHAFFER
SHANEFELT
SHANNON
SHARP
SHAULIS
SHAW
SHAY
SHEARER
SHELGEL
SHEPLER
SHERK
SHERRICK
SHERSEN
SHESSLEY
SHICK
SHIELDS
SHIPPECK
SHIREY
SHIREY (SCHEIRY)
SHIRLEY
SHOCKEY
SHOEMAKER
SHUPE
SHUTT
SICKMILLER
SIGMON
SILVEIRA
SILVIS
SIMMONS
SIMON
SIMPSON

SIPES
SKODAK
SLAGHT
SLATER
SLEZAK
SLOAN
SMALLY
SMELTZER
SMETAK
SMITH
SMITHLEY
SMITHLY
SNOW (SHOW)
SNYDER
SOMES
SOUDERS
SOUTHWELL
SOUZA
SOWARDS
SPANO
SPAYDE
SPEAKE
SPECK
SPENCER
SPICER
SPLENDOR
SPLITLOG
SPRINGER
SQUERI
ST. CLAIR
STABILE
STACY
STAFFORD
STAHL
STANFORD
STANISLAW
STANLEY
STARK
STARR
STATON
STAUFFER
STEELE
STEFFEY
STEIN
STEMPLE
STEPP

STEVENS
STEWART
STIENER
STIFFLER
STITT
STOEWHASS
STONE
STONER
STOREY
STOREY
(WOLLMANN-
STOREY)
STORMER
STOVER
STOWE
STOWELL
STRANAHAN
STREICH
STRETCH
STRIPLING
STROUP
STUART
STUMPT
STYNCHULA
SUGAR
SUMMO
SUPANCIC
SUTTON
SWANK
SWANSON
SWEENEY
SWIGART
SYSTER
TAIT
TALBOT
TALON
TARR
TAYLOR
TEASLEY
TEETS
TELFORD
TERRA
TESTA
THIEL
THOMAS
THOMPSON

THOMSON
TIGER
TIMMIONS
TINKEY
TITO
TOPINITSKY
TOPPER
TOSH
TRETTEL
TRIGG
TROTSHUL?
TROUT
TROVEN
TROXEL (TRUXAL)
TRUMP
TRUSKOWUSKI
TRUXAL
TURKEY
TURNER
TUSTIN
TWEEDY
UBER
UHLIG
UKISH
ULERY
UNDERWOOD
URBAN
URCH
UTO
VALE
VALENINTE
VAN WEY
VANDEL
VANHORN
VANSLUYTMAN
VARNELL
VAUGHN
VAVRO
VERWELST
VOGLE
WADE
WADSWORTH
WAGNER

WAHL
WALDEN
WALLACE
WALLBAUM
WALSH
WALTER
WALTERS
WALTHOUR
WALTHOUR-
MENSCH
WANO
WARDLOW
WARREN
WASH
WASHBURN
WATKINS
WATROUS
WATSON
WATT
WAUGAMAN
WEATHERALL
WEAVER
WECKERLY
WEDGE
WEGLEY
WEIMER
WEINRICH
WEISS
WELLER
WELLMAN
WELLS
WELSHONSE
WEST
WESTON
WHERRY
WHETZEL
WHIPPLE
WHITE
WHITECROW
(NUSLI)
WHITEWING
WIBLE
WIEDEMAN

WIGGS
WIKE
WILCOX
WILKENS
WILKINS
WILKINSON
WILLIAMS
WILLS
WILSON
WILT
WIMER
WINEGROVE
WINELAND
WINEMAN
WING
WINGERT
WINNEY
WITTEN
WITTENBURG
WOLFE
WOLLMANN
WOOD
WOODRUFF
WOODS
WOODY
WOOMER
WORTHAM
WRIGHT
WYANT
WYNN
YAMBER
YANITS
YINGER
YODER
YOHMAN
YOUNG
ZACUR
ZIER
ZILMORE
ZIMMERER
ZIMMERMAN
ZURICK
ZUZACK

NOTES

Chapter 1: While the Nicely family history handed down for generations indicated that my ancestor's homeland was in the Hesse Darmstadt region of Germany, this has changed with recent research and it is now confirmed that our original named ancestor Hans Knussli was born in the Canton of Zurich, Switzerland. The Knusli name has been spelled many ways over the years, partly due to being written phonetically on official records and phonetic translations. Following is a list of known spellings of the name. There are probably others not yet identified.

Crow	Knessly	Knysley
Kneisel	Kneuss	Knysley
Kneiseley	Kniceley	Nicely
Kneislei	Knicely	Niceley
Kneisley	Kniseley	Niesley
Kneislie	Knisely	Niesly
Kneisly	Knisley	Nisely
Kneissley	Knusli	Nisle
Kneissly	Knussli	Whitecrow

Chapter 3 and 5: The story of the capture of Jacob was reported in many different books over the years and the date of the capture was reported as 1790 or 1791. This was a date that was part of every report that I had read. If there was a date indicated in any of the family stories told to me, they had been long forgotten. The problem with this date was the birth record of a Jacob Kneisle born to Adam Kneisle Sr. in 1770. This date was recorded in the Harrold Zion Lutheran Church records. For many years in order for the 1790 date to be correct I assumed that the original Jacob had died and Adam and

Elizabeth gave the name of Jacob to their next male child who must have been born in 1785, in order to be five years old in 1790. However, I could not locate a birth record for a second Jacob. This was also puzzling since there was a birth record for Margaret in 1784 and Ann Elizabeth in 1786. Another problem with the 1790 date was that most of the problems with Indian raids appeared to have slowed near the end of the Revolutionary War in 1783. When the Whitecrow information reached me their information showed a date of 1778 for the capture of Jacob. Their information indicated he was 2 or 3 years old at the time of capture. At this point I made the decision to go with the actual recorded date of his birth and used the age of five as a basis for the 1775 capture date. This date could have varied by a year or two either up or down.

Another problem with the reported information had to do with the meeting in 1828. In spite of the fact the date of 1828 was pretty solid in both stories of the event, there also existed the possibility that the 1828 date was also in error. Later information received included an article in an Ohio newspaper that established the date as 1825. The major difference in the stories related to the visitor being Jacob's brother or his father. In the Nicely family version one story said it was a father and the other stated a brother went to meet with Jacob, while the Whitecrow family information and the information in the Ohio paper indicated it was Jacob's father who came to see him. The gravestone in Keltz Cemetery shows a date of 1826 for the death of Jacob's father Adam Sr. It would be unlikely at his advanced age of 95 to have made such a long journey on horseback. Since the Ohio paper indicated it was Adam who came to see him it was most likely his brother Adam Jr. This might have led to confusion in the newspaper account since his father's name was also Adam. In our family the story was always told that Adam Sr. had died without seeing his son and his mother died after finding out that he had survived the capture and prospered and had a family. Since Adam Sr. the father was alive in 1825 we assume the family history was not correct. We may never know the exact history on these actual events.

General Note: Family names or surnames were generally based on one of four categories: occupation, location, father's name, or characteristic. An example of an occupation would be a surname Miller for a person who was a grain grinder or a miller. A location surname example would be a John who lived over a hill became known as John Overhill. An example of a Father's name would be the son of a John became know with a surname of Johnson. Some examples of characteristic surnames would be Small, Large, Longfellow, or for a sly man, Fox. According to information given to me, the name of Knusli was a characteristic surname, which was the word for a short and stocky loaf of bread. In my case the short and stocky describes my body shape.

The results of the DNA testing discussed in the book can be viewed on the Family Tree DNA website under the Nicely Surname Project.

REFERENCES

Charles H. Glatfelter. *The Pennsylvania Germans. A Brief Account of their Influence on Pennsylvania*. Pennsylvania History Studies No. 20, The Pennsylvania Historical Association. University Park. Pennsylvania, 1990

Douglas MacGregor. *Native Americans and the Struggle for the Forks of the Ohio*. Westmoreland History, December 2003, Vol. 8, No. 3.

Floyd C. Eiseman, *Archibold Lochry, Loyalhanna Valley's Revolutionary War Defender and Martyr*. The Latrobe Historical Gazette, Fall 2000.

Jennifer Wilson. *The Rediscovery of Lochry's Blockhouse*, Westmoreland History, Summer/Fall 2000.

Microsoft® Encarta® Online Encyclopedia 2004, *Hessen*, http://encarta.msn.com © 1997-2004 Microsoft Corporation.

Shelby Miller Ruch. *One-Shot Prelude*. Westsylvania Stories, Westsylvania Corp., Vol. 7 No. 4 Winter '03/04

Steven M. Nolt. *A History of The Amish*. Good Books, Intercourse, Pennsylvania, 1968.

Thunderclouds of War Gather. Westsylvania Stories, Westsylvania Heritage Corp., Vol. 7 No. 4 Winter '03/04

ABOUT THE AUTHOR

Ronald Earl Nicely was born in Ligonier Township, Westmoreland County, PA, in his Grandfather's farmhouse on Nicely Road. He was the son of Robert Earl (Cappy) Nicely and Florence Rose McDowell Nicely. He was raised in the small town of Ligonier and spent many of his early years on the Nicely farm. He worked in garages and service stations after high school until he was drafted into the US Army in 1960. After his military service, Kennametal Inc. employed him for over 34 years. He earned a Bachelor of Science Degree in Business Administration from the University of Pittsburgh at Greensburg, PA. During the last twenty-five years of his Kennametal service he was a Business Forecaster.

After spending seventeen years in Raleigh, NC he returned to Latrobe, PA and began to research his family tree. This led to gathering not only the names but also the stories behind the members of his family tree. The capture of Jacob was especially interesting since he had heard the story early in his life from his Grandfather Charlie Nicely. Locating the original valley homesite and the capture site led to learning more about the history in and around the Four-Mile Run region of the Ligonier Valley. He resides in the Latrobe area with his wife of thirty-six years, Marian Chris Plummer Nicely. They have two children and one grandson.

He is a member of the Westmoreland County Historical Society and the Ligonier Valley Historical Society and serves as a volunteer docent at Historic Compass Inn Museum in Laughlintown, PA.

Made in the USA
Middletown, DE
17 March 2021